MY LIFE AS AN
Amish Wife

LENA YODER

HARVEST HOUSE PUBLISHERS
EUGENE, OREGON

Cover by Dugan Design Group, Bloomington, Minnesota

Published in association with Ridgeway Publishing, Medina, New York 14103.

All the incidents described in this book are true. Where individuals may be identifiable, they have granted the author and the publisher the right to use their names, stories, and/or facts of their lives in all manners, including composite or altered representations. In all other cases, names, circumstances, descriptions, and details have been changed to render individuals unidentifiable.

MY LIFE AS AN AMISH WIFE

Copyright © 2015 Lena Yoder
Published by Harvest House Publishers
Eugene, Oregon 97402
www.harvesthousepublishers.com

Library of Congress Cataloging-in-Publication Data
Yoder, Lena.
My life as an Amish wife / Lena Yoder.
     pages   cm
ISBN 978-0-7369-6423-4 (pbk.)
ISBN 978-0-7369-6424-1 (eBook)
1. Yoder, Lena. 2. Yoder, Lena—Family. 3. Amish women—Indiana—Biography. 4. Wives—Indiana—Biography. 5. Mothers—Indiana—Biography. 6. Amish—Indiana—Biography. 7. Amish—Indiana—Social life and customs. 8. Indiana—Biography. 9. Indiana—Social life and customs. I. Title
F535.M45Y63 2015
289.7092—dc23
[B]
                                                                        2015004706

Printed in the United States of America

15 16 17 18 19 20 21 22 23 / BP-JH / 10 9 8 7 6 5 4 3 2 1

Acknowledgments

My heartfelt thanks...

to God. Thank you for planting me in this community-rich, Amish settlement of Northern Indiana. Even when my family struggles, we are so abundantly blessed and surrounded by your love.

to my ever-patient and encouraging husband, Wayne. Without your support I would never come to first base. One of these days I will mend your pants again. Our 21 years of marriage have been *the best*!

to my children. You are our purpose in life. Thank you for being patient with me and all my whims. I would never survive without you. The Lord will richly bless you!

to the Connection *staff.* Thank you for letting me be part of your family for 10 years already. Without you, I would never have started writing.

Lena's Family & Friends

Wayne Yoder, husband
Lena Frey Yoder, wife
Colleen, age 13
Brian, age 11
Karah, age 8
Emily, age 6
Jolisa, age 4
Jesse, age 2

Grandma (Lena's mom)
Leanna, Lena's sister, married to Al
Sue, Lena's sister
Ida, Lena's aunt
Ida, Lena's sister
Grandma Raber, Lena's grandmother

A Note to You
from
Lena Yoder

I live on the 72-acre dairy farm I grew up on in the middle of a large Amish community. Together with my husband, Wayne, and our six children, we work our land and raise dairy cows.

One reason I want to share some of my daily life with you is simply to show you what the real Amish way of life is all about. With the proliferation of so many "Amish" TV shows, books, interviews, and stories that do not reflect our way of life, this true-to-life diary provides a glimpse of how we really live. Another reason I've offered this book is to show how Christ's love and strength help us through our daily lives. Like all Christians, we experience triumphs and struggles as we grow in our faith in Jesus Christ. "The joy of the LORD is [our] strength" (Nehemiah 8:10).

I've always loved anything to do with paper and pen. I've been scribbling on any available surface ever since I was a small child. All those scribbles led to starting a small business of artistic handwriting and acrylic painting. I do custom order projects for people in my community, as well as others. I've published two other books about life on our farm that includes many recipes from our daily menu.

Our main goal, as with any Christian family, is to live for Christ daily and let our light shine for him.

Year 1

Winter

Children are a great comfort in your old age—
and they help you reach it faster too.

This morning my 11-year-old son Brian wanted to take his hockey stick to school because *everybody* else has theirs there. There are several drawbacks. Number one is that he doesn't actually have one yet. He thinks we have one hidden away somewhere for his Christmas gift. The number two problem is that the pond isn't even frozen hard enough to play hockey yet. Oh, but everyone else has sticks there just in case! It seems so silly to us, but I remember how it used to be in school. It seemed we were always the "duh" ones. The sad part is that ugly peer pressure doesn't quit once you are out of school. However, I do believe as we get older and mature, we are able to pass it off better—if we choose to. I wonder how many of our adult pressures look as silly to God as our children's pressures look to us?

Right now I've got three little ones having a blast in the living room. They have their coats and scarves on and are pretending to be going to the fair. They have no idea what a fair is like, but they are having a blast. The living room pretty well looks like a fair too—imagine a hog pen. But the children aren't crying, and they are able to run, and jump, and play. We'll clean up later. These are the good days—busy and full of challenges, but we're all home, all able to help each other, and all able to enjoy each other.

Life on our farm was pretty well boring until the other morning when Wayne wanted a cow in the *head gate*.* [Definitions and explanations of words with *s after them can be found in the glossary at the end of this book.] Not being a die-hard morning person, I do not relish such endeavors. The cow decided it was not necessary to be forced into a place she did not long to be. I was appointed to stand in a little alleyway that leads to the *motor room*.* The cow was to go in exactly the opposite direction. She got downright evil as she came toward me and decided I was nothing to fear. She politely shoved me along, not worrying about the consequences she faced or where she was actually headed. She shoved me into the diesel room. I couldn't open the door to head on out because the door swings in, and she had me against the door. The room was dark, and she couldn't see. She promptly turned south *on* the motor block. She went clear to the end. Glass, pipes, bolts—you name it—were flying all over the place. I bailed out as soon as I could, sure that my husband wasn't happy with me. It was very icy at the time, so I slipped around outside a while, wondering how I'd gotten myself into this fix—now with another bill to pay with having ruined the motor. What if we can't even get it fixed today yet? I sure wish I could be anywhere but here.

But calmness took over Wayne, who was now getting the cow off of everything and assessing the damage done.

Shakily, I started picking up pieces and apologizing, wanting to say sorry and how worthless I really am a hundred times. I stuck with just a couple times because I knew that didn't impress him either. Luckily, Wayne can fix almost everything by himself, and no, the motor did not need to be replaced. He tried getting the cow in later that day by himself, but he finally gave up. We'll try some other time.

Too bad nobody is dropping in to do my mending. That's a job I push off way too long. Our everyday attire is pretty well rags. I need to sew myself new dresses. Then I'll wear what I have for good now as everyday ones. I always have a hard time throwing away old, worn-out clothing.

I'm known to recycle other people's clothing that doesn't fit anymore. I make little-girl dresses for my young daughters and pants for two-year-old Jesse. I've even made a quilt from dresses. I get a lot more use out of them than I would leaving unused clothes hanging in the closet.

◇◇◇◇◇

A couple weeks ago I went on an all-day Goodwill shopping trip. It was a treat because I had not gone for probably seven years. Wayne and I aren't anti shopping, but we don't endorse it either. Anyway, I enjoyed the day with neighbor ladies and got good deals on sweatshirts, boots, scarves, pillows, and such. The children had been hoping for some toys but were excited with the clothing and things I got.

Wayne was milking when I got home. The children were all excited to see me and the things I bought. I should've run for the barn to help Wayne. I should've held the little ones. I should've visited with the older ones. That is one big reason I do not go away a lot—because I cannot handle being torn apart like that. Where is my presence needed the most? In what direction should I fly? It is so much more peaceful if I just stay at home.

◇◇◇◇◇

I have three eager, smiling little faces right around the typewriter wanting to watch me. The children are full of questions and threatening to punch some buttons. Lunch will be ready in about 10 minutes, and then comes nap time, which means peace and quiet for me for quite a while. By the end of this sentence, they're already going their own way and playing nicely. Well, there's Jesse. He's content by himself as he's throwing my extra papers on the floor. I intervene when he picks up a little glass bowl to pitch to the floor from the chair he's standing on. Now he went to visit his grandma, who lives next door. Now he's back again. He is the pure definition of "busy."

◇◇◇◇◇

Jesse is surprising me by showing a real interest in going to the bathroom. Potty training is not one of my favorite jobs in parenting. Makes it nice when they actually want to. One of the first benefits little ones discover once they are out of diapers is that while sitting in church, if they decide they need a change of scenery, all they have to do is say, "I have to go potty!"

This forenoon, Wayne, the little ones, and I went to our community's private school a while. That is so inspiring to me. I wish I would take the time to go more often. Oh, to be filled with such youthful energy and eagerness! We have nine little first-grade girls (no boys) who brighten up that classroom as only sweet little first-graders can. With now being able to read, their little worlds are being opened up to so many fascinating new things. They were fun to watch. One wanted to show me that she lost one front tooth and the other one was loose!

With the first half of January being so warm and rainy we've, of course, had to deal with major mud here on our heavy-clay-soil farm. With that major mud comes the inability to haul manure, which causes a major messy barnyard. What can we do about it? Be patient and wait for it to freeze over or dry out, whichever one comes first. Remember, being patient means not complaining.

Last December we started a new venture in our farming business. We started milking three times a day. Actually, I should say Wayne does and I help. We milk in the morning at 5:30, Wayne milks in the afternoon at 1:30, and then we milk in the evening at 9:30. The first week and a half were rough going for me. My long, fixed schedule had changed and I, being a person who thrives on routine, had to adjust my patterns of doing things. I do see, though, that it has been very successful, and I am willing to continue on in this manner. There are definitely some drawbacks we have to swallow, but so far the good changes have outweighed the bad. The cows have responded far better than we had dared hope. I think this is less stressful than if Wayne would have gotten an off-farm job.

◇◇◇◇◇

On my kitchen windowsill I have a spring flower bulb partially submerged in water. The teachers gave it to us for Christmas. It's taking a long time to bloom but giving us hope nonetheless. I'm looking forward to the day it will give us blooms. This morning I broke the original glass vase it was in, and some of the root system was broken off. Hopefully it didn't do too much damage. I'm also eager to start all my tomato seeds. I'd like to start four varieties of non-acid plants along with the regular canning varieties.

We've butchered one beef for ourselves so far this winter. We want to do one more and also two small pigs. You're asking why so many? We just do younger, smaller beef and pigs, which gives us lean, quality meat.

With the one cow we butchered, I just canned chunks, and the rest was ground and put into the freezer. For the chunks, we put it through the large-blade grinder once, put it into cans (canning jars), added a teaspoon of salt, and pressure cooked it for 40 minutes at 10 pounds pressure. I like to use this canned meat for barbeque beef, beef stew, and beef and noodles. I'd love to use it for vegetable soup too, but I can't convince my family that's something they want to eat.

I will can fried steak and gravy, beef bologna, and more chunks when we butcher the next one. I put the bologna through the grinder at least three times after being mixed with seasonings for a much better tasting bologna with firmer texture. It doesn't taste so salty. The men like to doubt me, but it is a proven fact. I think I have convinced them all by now.

I look forward to having canned sausage links for breakfast too, and we make our own brats. These are all jobs I do not look forward to, but then it is so satisfying once we have fresh, good meat again. Praise the Lord for these precious blessings. We are blessed indeed.

◇◇◇◇◇

For a year now I have been working on improving my overall health—changing my eating habits, drinking more water, and getting body and mind refreshing exercise. I still have not conquered all my bad eating habits. That's probably something I will have to work at the rest of my life.

This forenoon I decided to bake a batch of chocolate chip cookies so the children have something to snack on. Like usual, Jesse had to be at the counter helping me. I turned my back to put trash in the wastebasket. Quickly he got an egg, cracked it open, and, surprisingly, got most of it into the batter bowl! The rest ended up on the front of the cupboard and on the floor. Whew, could have been worse.

Year 1

Spring

Due to the weather on Monday, our school was canceled for the day. That caused ripples of excitement throughout the house. I was even glad for the diversion to begin with. It was too nasty for Brian to be outside, so after chores and breakfast I got him started baking cookies. He didn't want ordinary chocolate chip cookies, but rather the soft, oatmeal chocolate chip that are rolled in powdered sugar. I told him regular chocolate chip would be easier. I was envisioning my powdered-sugar-coated kitchen by the time he got done. But then the kitchen is cleanable, so I got him going on the ones he wanted.

Karah and Emily were to wash the breakfast dishes and finish tidying up the house. I don't really know when the tidying up stopped and the messing up began. Between all that, I cut out a dress for Jolisa and got Colleen started on a sewing lesson. I spent most of the forenoon standing beside the sewing machine. Oh my, I do think I would make a better nurse than a teacher. It's easier for me to poke a child and bring him to tears than it is to teach something like basic sewing.

In reality, Colleen did really well. It's just hard for me to remember a time when I had to use my brain to control which way to treadle. It's been as natural as breathing for so many years now, and to see her pedal this way, then that way, and finally shoot forth in a crooked way is hilarious...or maybe frustrating. What is the word I'm looking for? I don't think it'll take long for her to catch on as she really wants to learn.

By the time Brian was done with the cookies and Colleen was almost done with the dress, it was high time for lunch. I made stew because everybody had so many cookies (they were delicious). I knew it would be useless to make a bigger meal.

I helped with the afternoon milking, and then Colleen and I baked two different kinds of cakes, made two pizzas, and got everybody ready to go away for supper. The children were very excited because we'd been home a lot lately, and they were ready for a change of scenery. We took supper to school for the teachers. It was a thoroughly enjoyed evening of eating, visiting, singing, and listening to some awesome harmonica playing. We came home, put the children to bed, and milked again.

Early Tuesday morning Jesse crawled into our bed, and I felt he had a fever again. He'd been battling a cold and cough since last Friday. I finally got him comfortable in his own bed, and he slept until 9:30. That's very unusual for him. I was done with the laundry before he woke up. I cut out seven dresses for the little girls by noontime.

Wednesday forenoon after chores, breakfast, going to the phone shack to check messages and make some calls, and getting mail ready, it was 9:30 by the time I got to the sewing machine. I got three blouses sewn before noon. I had plans to type in the afternoon. I got the typewriter, battery, and inverter all ready, and then the typewriter didn't work. I fiddled around with it for a while and finally called my boss at *The Connection* magazine, an Amish publication. In frustration, I poured out my sob story to her. I gave up that project for the day. Last fall I found a typewriter at a Goodwill store for $5 and was quite proud of myself...excited actually. Then the thing didn't work properly! So I borrowed my sister's typewriter, and now I've probably ruined it. Must have been in my sleep because I don't know when it happened.

We made an early supper of biscuits and sausage gravy, which is an all-time favorite meal for my family. The girls washed the dishes, and I went for a long walk. It was a beautiful evening, and I could refresh my mind. I came home and enjoyed the evening with the children. Wayne had gone to a meeting and came home late, so by the time milking was done we fell into bed at 11:30.

◇◇◇◇◇

Thursday I finished up the machine sewing on three dresses. It's taking way too long, but between settling many childish disputes, looking at farm magazines with Jesse, wiping runny noses dozens of times, fixing tea to drink with cookies—well, it just takes thrice as long to get something accomplished. I thought I had everybody happy with their tea and cookies, but it was mighty short lived. On the first or second dip of the cookie, Emily's fell in, so she had to have fresh tea. It wasn't a bother, as I just reused the same tea bag, but it was another trip away from the sewing machine. I couldn't convince her that those cookie crumbs sweetened her tea and made it even more delicious. Looked too much like cooties floating around in her cup to please her.

While I was sewing, Jesse had about a dozen small toy farm animals on the sewing machine to my right. I'd set them up, and then he'd play and knock them down. I'd set them up again. Next I had a pinched finger to kiss and blow on. Then he got dumped while flying around the house on his beloved, squeaky, red trike. Busy? Majorly. To have his sweet innocence...

◇◇◇◇◇

I'm longing for the warm, sunny days of summer. I think we all are. Summer spells freedom for me. I enjoy sewing in the winter, but I enjoy the vigorous, physical work of the summer even more. I like the busyness of spring planting, putting up hay, going on bike rides. Okay, I'll stop dreaming now...

◇◇◇◇◇

Not ready for school yet, Emily is the oldest at home during the day. We spend a lot of time together. She is a very good helper. She loves to color and write—anything that has to do with paper. She's starting to read a little, which is scary because she won't go to school yet this fall. Those are some of her good points.

She is also very picky and tries to act way above her age. She notices everything about anything and everybody, and it can be quite embarrassing for her mom sometimes. Talking about picky, the other day she had a banana to eat. It was a beautiful, delicious-looking banana. She peeled it and then stared at it a while.

"Mom, is this banana okay to eat?" she asked.

"Why, yes," I answered. "It's a good banana."

She took one bite. "Mom, is this tan stuff here all right to eat?"

"Yes, that's fine. That's just how a banana looks."

Another bite. "Mom, is this brown stuff all right to eat?"

"Yes, that's not brown. It's just darker than the outside, but its fine to eat." So on we go until she's finally eaten her banana.

Yesterday for lunch we had leftover baked chicken.

"Mom, is this brown stuff all right to eat?"

"Yes, that's just how chicken looks."

"Is this a bone or is it meat to eat?"

"Yes, Emily, that's meat, and it's okay to eat."

"Well, what's this dark-brown stuff?"

"It's blood vessels, and please just eat!"

The others don't even notice; they just eat.

I love to cook, and it's satisfying to feed a table full of hungry family members. I'm not as creative as I used to be because it seems I'm always pressed for time. I make soup again. We don't have soup as often as when I was growing up, but we had hot lunch in school every day. Here our children eat out of lunch pails for noon.

Recently I decided to be more creative and planned to make "Hearty Twice Baked Potatoes" and chocolate mousse pie. Duh me. I figured I'd use the potatoes we had on hand—not baking potatoes, but it would work the same. However, the things didn't want to get done. Finally I ended up scooping out the potatoes I could without ruining the shell too much. I cooked the insides a bit and then mashed them. I added cooked sausage, bacon, sour cream, shredded cheese, a bit of Italian dressing, salt, and pepper. I scooped it back into the shells and baked them again. It was plenty of work, but they were good. Next time I'd go about it completely different, plus I would omit the dressing and add more spices instead.

For a while I'd just been using regular baking flour for pie crusts because some other ladies said they do and like it. Well, I was just not satisfied and purchased pastry flour again. Using that and butter-flavored shortening makes the best crusts. Flaky and oh so good! I enjoy baking pies, but then I love to eat them too. They tend to jump immediately to my thirtysomething hips.

Anyway, this chocolate mousse pie was really simple and delicious. It calls for seven ounces of milk chocolate candy bar. I didn't have any, so I went over to Mom and Dad's rooms. They had two small bars, so I just added a handful of milk chocolate chips, until I figured I had seven ounces. It said to melt this chocolate with one-half cup milk and one-and-one-half cups miniature marshmallows (or 16 large). I went to the pantry to get them. Oh no! No marshmallows left. So again I borrowed from Mom. I cooked this mixture until smooth and melted. I stirred and stirred. Why don't all my chocolate chunks melt? I wondered. Emily reminds me that those candy bars from my mom had almonds in them. (Obviously I need more sleep.) I cooled the mixture, folded in two cups whipped whipping cream, poured all into a baked crust, and refrigerated for at least three hours. It was simple and delicious.

I also made a cherry pie for Wayne. I can easily leave that pie alone, but the apple pie I made a couple days earlier is harder to ignore—but I must. Now there's one pie crust left, and then it'll probably go quite a while before I get the urge again.

This forenoon I went to the house of a church lady for brunch to celebrate her birthday. There was brunch casserole, mixed fruit, cookies, and huge, picture-perfect blueberry muffins. Also finger Jell-O with milk and instant pudding in it. That was good too.

◇◇◇◇◇

It's high time for garden produce again, but I guess with our family I bake anyway, even with fresh fruits and vegetables available. I think that's part of our heritage.

◇◇◇◇◇

Last night coming in from *choring*,* I almost landed on the ground a couple times because of the mud. Our barnyard is terribly uneven from the freezing and thawing. The farm equipment leaves deep ruts, and with me almost sleeping, I have a hard time picking my feet up far enough to safely get me back to the house.

By the time I got into the house and showered, it was close to 11:20. I made a round upstairs checking on all the children, making sure they were still in bed and covered. What's sweeter than seeing your children peacefully sleeping?

◇◇◇◇◇

Today was just one of those days. I woke up with the flu, and when Mom doesn't feel good, well, it just doesn't go very well. I absolutely needed to do laundry, and it was a beautiful day to dry laundry outside. I thought I couldn't miss out on the spring sunshine. Colleen sorted the clothes before she went to school. Finally at nine o'clock I decided I might as well get up and at it. It took me until lunchtime, and I was exhausted by the time I got done.

Jesse threw up three times before breakfast, and I thought, "Here we go! It really is our turn to have this bug." Then he ate oatmeal and was fine after that. I didn't even look at the oatmeal. Maybe I should have. I hit the couch when laundry was all on the line and barked orders to the girls from there.

Emily made lunch for Wayne and the other little ones. It consisted of ham and lettuce sandwiches and some potato chips. She brought me her sandwich to show me how yummy it looked. She had two pieces of whole-wheat bread, Miracle Whip, a little bit of lettuce, and one piece of thin-sliced ham. I guess she choked hers all down because I didn't find any remains. Wayne had to smile at his. He didn't complain and ate it. She had used one pack of thin-sliced ham for all four sandwiches and had leftover meat. I would have used one pack per sandwich, especially for Wayne.

JoAnn, the girl who drives Colleen and Karah to school, wanted to talk with me when she dropped off the girls this afternoon. I opened the living-room window that faces the road to speak with her. All at once the window tilted in and fell down on my head. *Ouch!* The inside windowpane shattered from the impact. My thick head didn't shatter, but the crash did cause some stars to float around in front of me. Wayne wasn't too concerned about my head, but he did wonder how come I didn't go to the door instead of just opening the window. I felt like throwing a shoe at him because who would have thought the window would fall on my head? Oh well, I did get over it and decided not to harbor ill feelings.

Talking about laundry again...I think our towels look so drab on the lines. They are all the same washed-off color from 14 years of laundering. Now the other night my mother-in-law gave me a new pretty pink one, and it really brightens up the wash line! I do enjoy the simple, little things in life.

Emily and Jolisa often have to wash the dishes while I do the laundry. Jesse loves to help, and, oh my, what a mess they sometimes have. Jesse is usually very wet and sometimes the messes they leave behind make me wonder if it was worth it to get them to do dishes. Then the next time it goes better again, and I think they'll get it spotless one of these times.

◇◇◇◇◇

One day for lunch we decided we were thirsty for chocolate milk. Emily put the container of Nestlé's Quik on the table. I was busy with other lunch preparations. Jesse was quiet, and I was enjoying it—but I should have known better. All at once Jolisa said loudly, "Mom, look what Jesse did!" Nestlé's Quik was all over the table and floor. Having my back turned for a few minutes is all it takes for a busy little two year old. He's so busy, but oh how we enjoy the sunshine he casts on all our days.

◇◇◇◇◇

I have a brand-new walk-in pantry! Celebrate with me! There was just one door between our kitchen and my mom and dad's living room. Nothing against Mom and Dad, but it allowed us very little privacy. For seven years I dreamed of making a pantry at the end of their living room. The new pantry has two doors, one from our kitchen, and the other from their living room. It is nice and roomy with nice shelves, insulated walls, and room for the folding chairs, the sweeper, and so much more. It still allows us to get to my parents' from the inside, but also gives us so much more privacy.

◇◇◇◇◇

In December we lost a good workhorse mare to twisted gut. We had been looking forward to having her foal in early spring. Now Saturday night, we discovered her daughter, due to foal this week, was in distress. We had the vet out. He treated her and told Wayne he has to keep walking her and to not let her roll. It was close to 9:00 when the vet came, so at 9:30 I went out to milk. Wayne said I either had to keep walking Bunny or milk alone. I led her for a few minutes while Wayne put more clothes on. The decision was not a hard one for me to make. I would much rather milk 30 cows alone then lead one horse that's not supposed to lie down and roll, when that's exactly what she wants to do. Draft horse hooves are just too huge for my little feet—and in the dark to boot. Bunny didn't survive the night. It was a bitter pill to swallow. We had a good mother–daughter team that was very dependable. Must we have carried too much pride in them? We didn't think so.

Wayne gets the enjoyment of getting used to new horses we bought at a sale. It's a good thing the horse sale was right after losing Bunny because it's not a good time of the year to be without horses. Wayne talked me into going to the Topeka Horse Sale. I highly doubt I would be able to get him to go with me to a ladies convention with several thousand women present. I knew Emily, Jolisa, and Jesse would enjoy it, so I decided I'd go. It was okay as long as I was sitting, but climbing those bleachers trying to be halfway ladylike, trying not to fall, and trying to help the little children—well that just wasn't my cup of tea! I did get to visit with some people, and that made the forenoon worthwhile.

Year 1

Summer

Looking out my kitchen window as I'm washing the dishes, I see cows sticking their heads out barn doorways and lazily chewing their cuds. I enjoy seeing a green pasture with Holstein cows relaxing in the sun.

My girls flying around the circle drive on their bikes are having the time of their lives. Behind them comes Jesse on his trusty little red trike, putting all his effort into pumping those pedals as fast as he can. He rode that squeaky thing in the house all winter, and he's very attached to it. Riding it seems to be second nature for him. I enjoy the wonderful scenes of a gorgeous summer.

We are eagerly awaiting our favorite summer meals. Lettuce, radishes, onions, asparagus, berries, yellow squash, cucumbers, tomatoes...it takes long to prepare these summer meals, but can you tell me what is better eating? My thoughts ramble on to cooked red potatoes smothered with cucumber salad. I am beginning to hallucinate!

Our gas grill is a major appliance for us during the summer. We like to marinade chicken breasts in Italian dressing and then grill those for several minutes on a side. Those make some awesome sandwiches with fresh lettuce, onions, and tomatoes. During the summer, we generally have a meat, potato, and vegetable meal at noon, and then for supper we go light.

I am really enjoying these warmer days. We had two months

of the flu bug in our house, and it was time for a change of scenery. Brian, Emily, and Jesse were each sick for two weeks. They had earaches, headaches, and high fevers. Then Wayne got it. Oh my, it seems most women can identify with me that when the husband is sick...well, maybe it's best left unsaid. With having to keep the children's fever checked during the night, Wayne having a fever of 104.5, and milking three times a day, I was trying to survive with very little sleep. For three days I chored for eight hours. I gladly did it and everything went smoothly. Brian helped a lot too, as did a trusty farmer friend from church. The only other thing I accomplished that week was rubbing the children with *Unker's** on their chests, ears, backs, and bottoms of their feet. Wayne skipped eight milkings. What joy when he came to the barn again! Once he was back on his feet, I hit the sack and slept for quite a while. Wayne finally wondered, kiddingly, when the neighbors were going to come help him as they had helped me.

We're into the dust season again. With our house sandwiched between the gravel road and the barnyard, we just don't have much choice except eat dust. We do have our windows open unless it's extremely windy because I'd rather clean dust then breathe stuffy air. I love an open house with the curtains blowing in the breeze.

Wedding bells are ringing! I even get some new dresses for these grand occasions. Getting married is such a serious step to take, but if two young souls are one with the Lord and choose to be married, what a cause for celebration. In old Bible times they celebrated for days. I'm sure that parents now are glad we just have one-day weddings. It costs an arm and a leg the way it is, but it's well worth it.

This year Mom and Dad celebrated their fiftieth anniversary, my sister Leanna and her husband, Al, celebrated their twenty-fifth, and Wayne and I hope to celebrate our fifteenth in October. Actually there probably won't be a whole lot of celebrating as in going places and doing things, but there will be thanking the Lord for all his many blessings and praising him for allowing us to travel this way together for this many years.

◇◇◇◇◇

One Saturday this spring, Wayne encouraged me to go to the biannual Honeyville Consignment Sale with him. I agreed to go with the intention of getting a few bargains. A couple of other people thought so too. Our school has a lunch stand there each fall, so I know what it's like on that end of the deal, but I'm not used to the buying end.

I'm not one to take all my children to a babysitter, but this year they were old enough to stay at home. I thought I had too much work to do, but another part of me wanted to go. Brian and Jesse's bed have springs poking through, and each night when they went to bed we'd be gently reminded of it. Neither the boys nor the little girls have dressers in their rooms. I would love to purchase a new living-room suite, but in reality I knew I would be lucky to come home with anything at farmer prices.

That morning I started on the weekly cleaning, gave the girls some orders, and went out the door as if I had a great mission to accomplish. On the inside I felt immature and out of place. I was feeling like I would much rather stay at home and wash dishes and windows all day. It was a miserable day—cold and rainy, but it didn't seem to keep people at home, which is good because there were a lot of things to sell.

I spotted a couch I could've easily gotten used to in our living room, and also a bedroom suite with my name written all over it. I was nervous on bidding, but I tried to breathe deep and act mature. Somebody else wanted *my* couch too, so I gave up and let them have it. I did get a bedroom suite, but had to settle for the ugliest one there. Actually it's half-decent. I had to get some famous *Jones Fruit* * topped with the most delicious caramel and almonds. The children had also ordered kettle corn, so I got two bags before heading home.

The girls had the house ready to mop, so I quickly got that out of the way and started making plans for the rest of the afternoon. We put Colleen's old headboard and dresser into Brian's room. We pushed, pulled, and shoved Brian's old mattress down the stairs and out the front door. We emptied my old desk and heaved that out the door to join the rest of the outcasts out there. The drawers in that desk didn't work anymore, and it was just a place for the little girls to pile their treasures into instead of putting them into their proper places.

Next we brought the chest of drawers down from Colleen's room and put the desk things in there. Can you just imagine how our house of mix-and-match looks? Very livable, definitely not for show, but I hope visitors view it as inviting and comfortable.

With Colleen and Brian as my helpers, we took our box springs and mattress up to Brian's room and fixed his bed.

We finished up the cleaning and started supper. Wayne, Brian, and I went back to the sale to get our purchases and pay the bill. How exciting for the children (and their mama) to have something new.

Colleen quickly washed off the wagon dirt from the bedroom furniture, and then Wayne and I carried it inside. We got it upstairs, situated, and discussed. Colleen was tickled with the bedroom suite. It's a white one, and she wants me to paint daisies on the headboard and dresser. Wayne and I then put the new mattress set on our bed and fixed that. We released a huge sigh of relief. I also eliminated our head- and footboard to create more space in our teeny bedroom.

What a day! We ate supper at 7:00, and everybody was ready to hit the sack by then.

⬦⬦⬦⬦⬦

Sitting here at the kitchen table, I can see out the north, south, and west windows and enjoy scenes of the summer evening. I notice the hummingbird feeder needs to be replenished, and the two other bird feeders are empty also. I guess if there's nothing else to do around here, I can always feed the birds. As if I have nothing else to do.

I can see the green garden. The produce is flourishing with all the sunshine and moisture. The east part is freshly tilled as we planted the potatoes tonight. I decided to plant the potatoes later this year to see if we can get a better crop...and also to see if they keep better through the winter. Last year's crop was a total failure. Every time I bought potatoes at the store during the winter I was embarrassed. To me, planting enough potatoes to last most of the year is part of our heritage. I realize some basements are too warm and the potatoes spoil, but I really appreciate crates full of potatoes in the basement. It gives me a strong sense of working together with the Lord to supply for my family.

Colleen fertilized both gardens and flower beds this morning as Wayne, Brian, and I chored. After breakfast Karah and Emily were supposed to pick potato bugs. It's hard to keep them at that job. Karah finally put a pesticide on the plants, but I honestly think that's a treat for the bugs. We keep on battling.

Next Karah and Emily were supposed to pick up Jesse's toys and Sam's debris from the yard. Sam is our three-and-a-half-month yellow Lab-mix dog. He looks like a full-blooded Lab. Colleen and Brian had been watching the pet ads in the papers and luckily noticed this ad. They'd been aching for a Lab, and here were some advertised for $20! Their dog fever ran plenty high. We've been pleased with him so far. Of course, he is still in the puppy stage, and I've had to replace some plants.

Jesse and Sam are best buddies. Jesse is usually up early and goes outside to visit and pet Sam, crooning "Hey, Sam, hey, Sam," in his cute two-year-old talk. The two are fun to watch. As a small pup, Sam looked like the puppy on the wrapper of Cottonelle toilet paper.

Back to our gorgeous day. Brian ran the weed-eater most of the forenoon. Colleen baked chocolate chip cookies, which are everybody's favorite. Then she moved on to mowing the lawn. I sprayed for weeds. Between trying to keep everybody busy, taking Jesse to the bathroom, and applying a Band-Aid to Jolisa's foot, I deep-cleaned the porch. The porch is a small but vital room in our house. I washed the walls, woodwork, furniture, and rearranged a bit. I also cleaned out the girls' toy box, cleaned the roller shades, and swept the floor.

Colleen grilled hamburgers, and I made mashed potatoes and sweet corn for lunch. We skipped the normally present garden salad and served applesauce. Fresh strawberries and cookies for dessert. After our noon siesta, Colleen finished mowing the lawn, Karah swept the kitchen, and I washed the dishes. The four little ones and I took strawberry jam to our freezer kept at our neighbors. They have a freezer from which they sell treats. We took money along and bought pop and ice cream for everybody. The children all loved it, and it was worth the messy faces their mama had to wash.

The next 14 working days will look much like today—filled to the brim with getting ready to host church services here. This is a time of deep-cleaning, which I look forward to. Too bad it doesn't stay clean for a longer period of time, but such is life.

I'm working on blooming where I'm planted...if I don't fall asleep on the couch and entirely miss the 9:30 PM milking. This phase in my life has given me a whole new dimension on being submissive to my very loving husband. I feel like ranting and raving about milking three times a day, but I have no right. I need to work on cultivating my small spot in this world every day. I have a hard enough time deciding what to make for lunch, so you know how deep my brain waves go. In all seriousness, Wayne is very supportive of me and my whims. He would never force me into helping him. He makes me *want* to help him (except the 9:30 evening milking). I feel very privileged to have my whole family home working and playing together. How very, very blessed we are.

The last two months I've filled in every once in a while for Wayne at the 1:30 milking so he could work in the fields or get the hay in. Brian usually helps me, and I really enjoy it. Except on the day when the feed man stops in and everything goes wrong. By the time he leaves, the *milking parlor** looks like an outhouse, and I feel like a failure. Oh well. I have no desire to try to impress him, but why do things always go haywire when someone else is around? Such is the life of a farmer's wife.

◇◇◇◇◇

One day last week Wayne and Brian went fishing. A first-time experience for Brian in his almost 12 years of living. He thought it was pretty grand. They drove 12 miles to my brother Jay's house, and then he took them another four miles to the lake. Karah, Emily, and Jolisa rode along to spend a day with their cousins Lisa and Anita. The house was quiet here at home with just Colleen, Jesse, and me. We could've easily just had sandwiches and chips for lunch while sitting on recliners, but Colleen wanted fresh red potatoes, cucumbers, and kohlrabi, and I wanted fresh green beans.

It would be easy to eat as a vegetarian these beautiful summer days with all these delicious garden goodies. We've been eating yellow summer squash—lots of it. They produce like crazy, and we can't eat them fast enough even if we ate some every day. We love them with bread and butter or just as a vegetable. The little ones eat them as fast as we fry them.

Our romaine lettuce has been so-o-o-o good this year. Sinking my teeth into a huge piece of homemade bread thick with Miracle Whip, romaine lettuce, and salt is so good! I pile the lettuce on about an inch thick with absolutely no guilt.

I have a long, thick row of rooster-comb flowers in the garden. Their bright-red color adds dimension to the green foliage of the vegetables. There is a patch of voluntary sunflowers in the midst of the potato patch cheerily showing their faces to passersby. They too add character and color to the garden, making it a joy to look at.

The keeper potatoes need fertilizer. I used dry fertilizer when we planted, now I need to spray them with a *foliar**. We did that with the red potatoes, and they look really nice. Hopefully they'll produce whopper potatoes and not just be all show with beautiful foliage.

We're really enjoying the blooms of the miniature hollyhocks we can see from the kitchen window. I'm convinced I'll save those seeds and plant them for years to come.

The other day I went to the garden to gather our noon meal with Jesse tagging along. He wanted to help me pick green beans. He had his own pail and wasn't impressed at all if I picked too fast. He wanted his own share, which took long.

I'm also canning green beans, and I want to do the red beets and start on the pickles pretty soon. Next week we want to go pick blueberries. What we don't eat fresh, I will make into pie filling and can it. This week I've canned 30 quarts of black raspberry pie filling. That was fun because I know what a treat that is to prepare in all kinds of delicious dishes—pies, cheesecakes, and *Long Johns**! Remember me saying I'm changing my eating habits? I really do watch what I eat and only fix these treats occasionally—tasting only a little to satisfy my sweet tooth.

Yesterday Colleen, Brian, and I went out to the west garden to clean it. We have two gardens and call them the "east" and "west" gardens because of where they are located. What fun to go out together! The work didn't take long at all with three of us. We don't need to clean the east garden this week. With the corn so tall, it pretty well takes care of itself. We also have raspberries and asparagus in that garden. I'm discouraged about the raspberry plants. I'm afraid one of these times I'm going to reach the point of just getting rid of them. I really don't want to, but I'm tired of cleaning the patch without greater returns. Most of the raspberries I canned this year I got elsewhere.

◇◇◇◇◇

Saturday night we had visitors for the night. We were having a meaningful chat close to midnight, when all of a sudden the noise level went up several notches. We had us some high-strung excitement! I guess we'd outstayed our little furry friends' regular visiting hours. Talk about embarrassing, but they definitely created some memories. Just that day Wayne had replenished their "feed" supply in the basement because we had spotted some evidence of their presence. Hopefully they experienced some pretty bad tummy aches since. We haven't seen them since. I guess that's part of the joys of living in an old house with crumbly, old, stone basement walls and easy entry holes all over for pesky field critters. We usually do have pretty good control over them, but seemingly in the fall they search for warmth...only to meet untimely deaths. In reality, our house is quite cozy and inviting, although small compared to most residences in our community. It is quite functional for our family. I love keeping my home clean and inviting to all who enter—especially to those who live here every day. I want it to be a place of quiet and clean refuge from the world surrounding us.

Year 1

Fall

We have been enjoying our beautiful North Indiana August. In all of my 34 years of living, I do not recall ever having such pleasant August weather. Fifty-degree nights in the dog days. I could live with these all 12 months of the year. I'm trying to enjoy this week to the absolute fullest because school will start on Monday. We'll have to change our schedule again for the next eight or nine months. The summer flew by. Too bad we don't have school for four months and summer vacation for eight months.

The sweet corn is in the freezer. The job was made sweet this year because two of my friends came and helped me. We did corn two days in a row: one day at Esther's house, the next day for me. Every year the children can help more, and the responsibilities change. Sometimes it takes a whole lot of bossing, and it would be a lot easier to do it by myself, but I've decided I want to teach them while they are young. Now, to keep myself disciplined and focused on my goals.

We canned a lot of garlic dill and kosher dill pickles this summer. We did the kosher dill first because we didn't have any left in the base-ment, and the children can hardly wait to have some again. What are grilled hamburger sandwiches without kosher dill pickles? We eat them with any hot or cold sandwiches.

We've also canned green beans, red beets, blueberry pie filling, and black raspberry pie filling. I'm not halfway through canning season, and my big helpers will be off to school.

◇◇◇◇◇

Today we were off on an adventure. We all went to the Shipshewana Flea Market. There weren't as many people on the grounds as there are sometimes, so it wasn't too bad with the children in tow. I learned a valuable lesson, and it still grinds me to a T. The first row we went down included a stand with good bedsheets for $20. I thought it was a good price, and I've needed a set for quite some time already. I always thought the good sets at Walmart were too expensive, and that next time they might be on sale. Now here they were for $20. The guy said he was the only one here selling these...blah, blah, blah. So I bought a set. Well, we hadn't gone too far when we came upon another stand with the exact same sheet sets for $14.95! We probably saw six to eight different places that were selling them for $14.95. I know I could have taken mine back and gotten one elsewhere, but I decided I'd just take this as a lesson. The next time I'll go several aisles before jumping for a deal.

I see all types of people at the flea market. Pale, dark, big, small, happy, unhappy. I always feel very conscious about being courteous, cheerful, and friendly. I try to let my light shine. A lot of people there know little of us [the Amish], and I wish to convey a Christian attitude.

We got our winter supply of booties for the girls and Jesse to wear in the house this winter when the snow flies. We also bought watermelons and peaches—some of our favorite fruit. Our watermelons in the garden aren't ripe yet.

I treated the children to pizza, which we all greatly enjoyed. We crossed the road to Spector's Dry Goods to buy a bonnet for Colleen. It was deemed very necessary as she says she's been wearing the same one since second grade. She's ready for the eighth grade now! We got our money's worth out of that one. It was a black outer bonnet that she wore to and from school. It's actually still in good shape, and I'm sure one of the other girls will wear it now.

After coming home, Colleen and I did the laundry. It looked like rain, and it did sprinkle for a while. We could easily use a good soaker, so I wouldn't have complained had our laundry gotten wet.

◇◇◇◇◇

Wayne milked after Brian had prepped the parlor. Brian mixed some feed in the *TMR* or *mixer wagon.**

I gathered some tomatoes and cucumbers for supper, peeled peaches, cooked filling for fresh peach pie, and did other odds and ends. While walking through the garden to gather vegetables, I had a hard time accepting how fast it is emptying. Made me sad.

After supper the three little girls and I went on a walk. Actually, I walked and they rode their bikes. I'd prefer to go alone, but for some reason they love to go along and talk and talk and talk. Sometimes I long for quiet, but they won't be little for long so I try to swallow my selfishness.

We're anticipating the Honeyville Consignment Sale this weekend. Emily and Jolisa get to go along on Friday for a while, and they are excited. Our private school has a lunch stand there on Friday and Saturday. With a team effort, we sell several thousand sandwiches, plus French fries, root beer floats, soft-serve ice cream, and drinks. We see a lot of people—unless we're bent forward making sandwiches like crazy.

◇◇◇◇◇

Our yellow lab, Sam, is such a people dog. Jesse likes to play horse with him. He puts a rope in his mouth and leads him around pretending Sam's our Belgian horse Jordan. Jesse says Sam's a high-stepper.

◇◇◇◇◇

On August 17, my mom had a stroke in the buggy on the way home from church. We summoned the ambulance, and they took her to the hospital. From there she was life-flighted to a bigger hospital. She was unresponsive for a couple days.

"Is any sick among you? let him call for the elders of the church; and let them pray over him, anointing him with oil in the name of the Lord: And the prayer of faith shall save the sick, and the Lord shall raise him up; and if he have committed sins, they shall be forgiven him" (James 5:14-15). We actively practice this by calling the ministry to gather to pray, anoint, and sing together (if requested). So on Thursday evening, August 21, she was anointed, and it was a miraculous experience. We had been unable to awaken her, but about halfway through the ceremony she woke up and seemed to know what was happening. Later she didn't remember, but that didn't matter.

We were at the hospital in Fort Wayne for 10 days, and then she was moved to a rehabilitation facility in Goshen called The Maples. During this time Mom would fall into a deep sleep, a result of her stroke. Some days she knew who we were; other days it seemed she didn't.

On August 30, one of our beloved neighbor ladies died. It was a very emotional week for me, especially because Mom didn't seem to comprehend. The lady and her husband were neighbors for all of Mom's 72 years of life. At the same time, our closest neighbor lady was in the hospital gravely ill with an infection, and their newborn son was in another hospital. On August 27, a neighbor man fell at work, but he was treated and released. Still caused us a scare. On September 8, another neighbor man fell at work and was in the hospital until September 18, when he passed on to eternity. He was 44 years old and left a wife and six children.

Mom had more strokes and seizures from September 10 on, until her passing on September 14.

The past month has been such a sad time for us, but we have countless blessings to thank our Lord for. I cannot imagine living without community and church support. My heart is broken, as are my family's hearts and the hearts of the rest of the church people. Three funerals in three weeks' time. I trust the Lord in all his ways, and he will heal our broken hearts.

◇◇◇◇◇

How I struggle with missing Mom and the kids missing their

grandma. Our houses are attached, so our children spent many hours with her. I struggle with the fact that my youngest children won't really remember her. Sure, they'll remember how she looked, but not the person I knew. Time has gone around long enough that we have found a new normal. And then something happens that throws me for a loop, and I need to refocus again. I do find that talking about Mom's stroke, death, viewing, funeral, and all the happenings at that time is a comfort to me. It will remain a mystery to us what exactly Mom could comprehend during that month. Sometimes she would surprise us by what she said, but she never seemed to remember anything for more than a minute or two. Jesse could usually get a bigger response out of her then the rest of us.

On the home front, the neighbors pretty well took care of us with food, babysitting, chores, canning tomatoes...the list could go on. The goodness of our friends' hearts is overwhelming to me. We are truly blessed.

Since all we've had going on, the three youngest have been extremely clingy. That's stating it quite mildly. Sometimes they almost drive me crazy, but I know they don't know how to cope with their loss. Sometimes I seem helpless in trying to help them. They had spent many hours with their grandma and must now deal with living without her.

I need to sew some thick winter coats before it gets too cold. I've done one and need to make at least five more. Sure wish I could find some cheap, double-faced lining somewhere. Buying lining for so many coats is very expensive. At least the coats are usually worn a number of years, so if I divide the cost over the years it's not so bad.

All the children need clothes, and I'd love to sew several quilts and do some painting projects this winter so I won't be entertaining boredom at all. Each winter I think I'd like to make enough greeting cards to last a year. Each winter comes and goes, and I never get it done. Maybe this year...

Year 2

Winter

I actually got to cross some things off my list of things to do today. It seems to take me way too long to accomplish anything these days. Baking, cleaning, laundry, and those everyday pleasures seem to take up most of my time. I have a habit of not giving those jobs any credit on the "to do" list.

I finished a coat for Colleen and redid my thick winter coat that made me look like I belonged to a football team. I sewed in the side seams a good two inches—a bonus of changing my eating habits. I also sewed Jesse a white Sunday shirt. Last week I sewed Jolisa a much-needed, long-sleeved dress. The first time she wore it, she ripped a little slit in the skirt. Her dress caught on the buggy step as she was crawling off. Sometimes I'm pretty sure nobody else has this ruckus when they're getting ready to go somewhere or when going home. Our extended families all live good distances away, so we're always in a hurry to get on the road. Making sure the little ones use the bathroom *before* they're dressed in their coats, scarves, and mittens is a job. Actually they have gloves this year, so we need to get all the fingers and thumbs in the right places. Then finally everybody is out the door except me. I always feel so fresh and sweet after hurrying around so much.

You're asking why we don't allow more time to get ready? You tell me because I don't know. That's just the way we are. I rarely go away with a messy house, so it's my own fault, I guess. That's a trait I learned from my mom. We'd never go to bed or away with any clutter or dirty dishes around. I was one of the youngest, and by that time most of my siblings were married or on their own. That meant Mom wasn't as busy so she could keep a tidier house than before.

When my family gets home and everybody is tired and half asleep, I really question why I wanted to go out in the first place. The children are all old enough to put their wraps away now, but they still need reminders each time. Maybe someday they'll remember.

◇◇◇◇◇

I'm multitasking again. Colleen wants lessons in calligraphy, and Emily wants reading lessons. The little girls are making bookmarks, and they want my input every once in a while. Jesse is on the table threatening to touch the typewriter to see what happens. Jolisa is humming "I Want to Stroll over Heaven with You." Colleen and Brian are humming a song they don't even know the name of. It's a song somebody put on our voicemail. Wayne went to the men's singing practice tonight so everybody is vying for Mom's attention.

◇◇◇◇◇

This fall when Wayne took the boys to the Topeka Horse Sale, the girls and I raked leaves. The girls were amazed at the beauty of the leaves, which reminded me of a craft project we used to do in school. Karah shaved crayons with a pencil sharpener, and then we put a couple pretty leaves and sprinkles of crayon shavings between two layers of wax paper and ironed it to melt the shavings, which gave it a stained glass effect when the sun shines through. Next on the list will be making paper chains and snowflakes to hang around the house for the holidays.

◇◇◇◇◇

The children's practicing of their Christmas program takes me down memory lane to my days at Honeyville School and having our programs. I'm thankful our children are taught more meaningful songs now than what we learned in public school. I have many wonderful memories from being on those creaky risers and that old stage with Mrs. Holmes as our teacher. Now I can imagine all the stress she endured trying to guide our boundless energy in the right direction. I remember being Jesus' mother, Mary, one year and nearly melting in those warm robes we wore. Being one of the angels with shiny wings and a golden halo was always special too.

Colleen just now modeled her new coat for me, and I'm convinced I made a huge mistake. I decided to get the cheaper one-sided lining to make the coats, and I shouldn't have. These coats are very bulky. They look like they're stuffed with marshmallows.

◇◇◇◇◇

Butchering season will be different this year for our family as Mom always helped, but now we only have precious memories. I am thankful we made memories together.

◇◇◇◇◇

I promised the little ones I'd read to them once I'm done writing— if they straighten up the house first. It didn't take them long to clean up, and now they are walking through the house with a bad case of the giggles mixed with coughs, yells, and way-too-loud talking. What fun they are having. Jesse even forgot his little farm toys for a bit.

◇◇◇◇◇

Saturday night Wayne cooked a double-batch of cornmeal mush. Sunday we shared the fried mush with my brother Jay, his family, and my dad. We had leftovers Monday and Tuesday morning. Colleen thought we could have some every morning, but I disagreed. We eat it with sausage or tomato gravy. We'd all soon be roly-poly if we ate it every morning. That's one of our favorite winter meals though. I'm thankful I was taught to cook in a wholesome way, even though we enjoy many modern dishes too—tacos, burritos, oriental salads, calzones, to name a few.

It's Saturday afternoon, and the weekly cleaning is pretty well done. The girls are washing the dishes and mixing a batch of party mix. This forenoon Colleen and I did the cleaning and canned 14 quarts of beef bologna. Then at 11:00, a family friend from Kalamazoo, Michigan, picked me up to go out for lunch in Shipshewana. Two of my sisters, my sister-in-law, and I enjoyed a very leisurely lunch and a bit of shopping with our friend. That was a very rare treat and made me wonder why we sisters don't do something like that more often.

The little girls are moaning and groaning because I said once the dishes are done we'll need to wash their hair. That's about the biggest thorn in their lives at this age. They have long, thick hair, and it's a major deal because they dread it so much. I remember when I was young and Mom would wash and comb my hair. It's a wonder I have hair and a forehead left! It always felt like she was pulling out all my hair and skinning my forehead. It seemed she'd pull my eyebrows up an inch by pulling my hair back so tight to braid it. I'm sure it wasn't nearly as bad as it seemed to me at that time. It does give me compassion for my girls now.

I don't braid my girls' hair. I suppose that's sort of a lost art. My friends in Jamesport, Missouri, braid their girls' hair, and I'm in awe at their talent. Teeny braids all over their heads that keep their hair very neat. Never having pursued that art, it's much quicker for me to put the girls' hair in buns.

When I was young, I was often ridiculed about all my scribbles on anything and everything that had a blank space. I thought space was just begging to be written on. Well, now I have three little girls who also love paper and anything that goes with it. Emily and Jolisa especially so, with Jolisa being the worst. She loves to collect any trash mail, envelopes, advertisements, calendars—you name it, she stashes it. I think I kind of know how my siblings felt about me. It takes a lot of paper to keep my girls satisfied.

◇◇◇◇◇

The other week I got this crazy idea to bake some cinnamon rolls. That's a rare occasion for me because I'm not very good at it. The process went pretty well, and I was marveling at how nice they looked in the oven. I was taking the first pan out of the oven and probably feeling a bit too smug because the next thing I knew the pan jumped out of my hands and fell onto the open oven door and oven racks. *Kerplop!* Down went my beautiful cinnamon rolls. Down went my pride. I didn't even realize I was feeling pride, but I must have been. Why else did it have to happen? With all the air poufed out of them, the rolls looked like total failures. I gathered the globs of dough together and pitched them back into the pan. After they were cooled, I frosted the "things" and we ate them. The rest of the pans weren't too bad, so we actually got to enjoy some that looked like what they were supposed to be.

Talking about flops, for quite a while I hid two cans of Pepsi in my undies drawer, saving them for a treat one night for Wayne and me after the children were in bed. When the time was right, I fixed each of us a glass of ice, brought them into the living room, and proceeded to open the first can. We both coughed at the appropriate time in hopes the ears upstairs wouldn't hear. Just as I opened it, the can fell from my hands and hit the rug. Believe me, I can move fast if I have to, but it wasn't fast enough to save my Pepsi or the rug. *Groan.* Needless to say, we shared a pop. Served me right to not share with the children, but then two cans of pop wouldn't have gone very far.

I don't know what the Lord is trying to tell me, but it seems he's trying to tell me something with all the flops I've been having.

I spent three days working on head coverings. I ended up throwing five out of the eight away, and the others are only good enough to wear at home. They all turned brown, tan, beige, or whatever ugly color a person wanted to call them. I saw red...and then I kind of saw mud...through the tears I shed in pure frustration.

I do have good moments too. Just now Jesse looked up from his play and said, "Hi, Mama!"

And I baked cinnamon rolls again this week, and they turned out okay. They're still not like I dream of making, but they are edible.

Another good happening was on Thursday when we butchered a beef. Three of my siblings and two in-laws came to help. I gladly sent some fresh meat home with them because we really appreciated their help. I canned 27 quarts of chunks, 60 quarts of bologna, and there are two 13-quart mixing bowls of steaks waiting to be fried and canned. I also make pan gravy to can with the steaks. It's a job I dread, but I love the privilege of going to the basement and having these blessings at my fingertips.

Jolisa had wanted to go out to the shop to see the freshly dressed beef that night, but before she quite got to the shop her little legs hurt so badly she just couldn't go a step further. Poor thing just had to come to the house. By the next day it must not have looked so mean anymore because she dared to enter the shop, spending some time out there watching us work.

Zero degrees and the snow is coming down fast. Colleen, Brian, and Karah are off to school. Emily and Jolisa are washing the breakfast dishes, and Jesse is squeaking through the house on his trusty red trike. He has two different kinds of socks on because something swallowed the matching ones. He's happy, often singing or blabbering to himself. It's amazing what all a little three-year-old mind can remember, especially songs and small poems, in a language they don't even really understand.

We're keeping our house cozy this winter with our coal stove in the kitchen and a small gas stove in the living room. Last year we had such a problem with our coal stove that it almost caused me anxiety attacks and a huge dread for this winter. Now we've not had any such problems this winter. The fire hasn't gone out once. Last year if we didn't stoke the fire every three hours the thing died on us, so we could plan on coming home from church, town, or wherever we went to a cold house and the frustration of starting it up again. I am ever grateful that it is better this year.

Jesse has the china cabinet door open again—but not for long! For some reason the four youngest think that's a wonderful place to store their treasures. I find anything from loose change to empty gum wrappers, from cut-out advertisement papers to bookmarks, from small purses to you name it and it's probably there. I guess they know that's where I keep my untouchables, so they want theirs there too. Every once in a while I'll make some disappear, and they never even ask about it, so must be the value diminishes with time.

◇◇◇◇◇

I'm still debating whether I want to start my own flowers from seed this year or not. I'd love to, but my porch table is full of quilt pieces and I really don't have room anywhere else. I have geraniums in the basement, and it's a bit late already to start flowers from seed, so I'd better make up my mind.

I will do vegetables though. That's no question at all. I've saved seed from last year. Actually, I'm trying the method of putting slices in dirt. I'll start watering them in February and see what happens. I used to send for my seeds, but now I prefer going to the local garden center and buying there what I do not save of my own. I like the idea of patronizing local businesses that put their hearts into serving us.

I am thoroughly enjoying these winter days at home. I've actually been piecing some quilts for my sister Leanna. I grew up quilting, and I'm convinced it's in our blood as all us sisters like it.

Next week I'll have to sew Brian some Sunday pants. He says his are so tight pretty soon they'll lift him off the ground. Probably true. Will have some sewing to do for the summer, but I don't have any fabric on hand, so for now I will enjoy doing the quilts while I have the chance.

Along with the enjoyment of sewing the quilts comes the sheer delight of receiving cash once they are done. But then that causes me more anxiety because there are so many things I'd like to do with it. I don't know what is the smartest or most beneficial choice to make for the whole family. Poof! Then it's all gone, and I don't have to think about that anymore. Smiles!

◇◇◇◇◇

We're still milking three times a day. Yes, we are. I'm looking forward to when Colleen is out of school. Colleen, Brian, and I can then trade off on the afternoon milking to relieve Wayne.

We've had half a dozen or so fresh cows lately, which helps. Wayne says more on the way.

◇◇◇◇◇

Sam the dog is spoiled rotten this winter. Wayne lets him sleep in the porch entrance. In the morning the dog goes out to chore with me. He likes to be in the parlor at every milking—drinking milk and aggravating the cats.

Wayne has tamed some of the cats out there, and one does not get along with Sam at all. I am not a cat person at all, but I can tolerate them because they've been good against the mouse population around there. We all enjoy Sam even though I sometimes get huffy when Wayne or one of the children feed him cookies or other food still fine for human consumption. Spending hours baking cookies is not one of my favorite things to do, so if I catch someone feeding fresh cookies to Sam, they'll have Mama to deal with. I don't know which is cheaper—store-bought dog food or home-baked cookies. Probably the cookies, unless I figure in my time. Mom's aren't supposed to figure in their time, I know. Surely it's okay though—if it pertains to a dog. I know which is healthiest though, so we'll continue to buy dog food.

Year 2

Spring

I'm enjoying a beautiful day! While hanging out the laundry this forenoon, I heard the birds singing their songs. My favorites to listen to right now are the red-winged blackbirds because of what their message means to me: Spring is on its way!

When I went to join Wayne in the barn this morning, the moon and stars were magnificent sights to behold. The sight brought my thoughts to our Savior once again—the Creator of these wondrous sights.

I also thought of the laundry. Looks like a gorgeous day to dry laundry out on the lines...in the sunshine and the breeze. After a long winter of drying nine people's laundry on top of the coal stove in the kitchen and the gas stove in the living room, it will be fun to hang it all outside again. I enjoy doing laundry more with the children a bit older and not having as many interruptions. Just once this forenoon while I was at the lines I heard Jesse calling for me. I settled a bunch of squabbles while in the washhouse though, but so it goes. I have a habit of turning around and looking at the lines once everything is hung up and I'm on my way to the house. I feel satisfied and thankful for the clothes, the towels, the soap, the water, and the health and the strength to do the job. All on such a beautiful day!

Once I was done with the laundry, the children wanted oranges and apples, so we sat around the table and had a little break. Jesse and

I stirred together a batch of buttermilk cookies and set it outside to chill and bake later on today. I don't bake "roll out" cookies too often because I think I'm in too much of a hurry, but I was hungry for some of Mom's cookies. I needed to bake cookies to take along to my grandma's tonight anyway, and then we'll have some for ourselves for a few days.

◇◇◇◇◇

This morning while doing chores it was hard to keep my spirits up and focused on my blessings. Two of our too-few cows are beyond any good anymore. We need to get rid of them today. A heifer got one of her teats frozen, and ever since we've been trying to get that better. It takes a long time to milk her and about more patience than we've got. Then we discussed the fridge again. The thing doesn't work well, and new ones are so expensive. Then I think the Lord knows and he cares—I just don't always understand his ways.

The milk price plummeted to extremely low again. We'd promised ourselves we wouldn't put ourselves through this again, that we would simply quit milking and do something else. Now what else is there to do? With no other jobs available, we have no choice. We don't want to quit, but it looks so hopeless. We can't afford to go on, but we can't afford to quit either. It would be so easy to despair, but that is what Satan wants us to do. So we try to wait patiently and see what God has in store for us.

I try to remember that patience includes the quality or habit of enduring without complaint. That makes me turn red in the face and squirmy, with my hands covering my face. I fail miserably.

◇◇◇◇◇

It's now six months since I had a real conversation with Mom. You know, grief isn't just missing her and getting used to life going on without her. Grief affects every aspect of my life. Some days it makes me crabby, some days I'm weepy, most days I'm tired. I deal with things differently, and I think it's all influenced by grief. I knew losing a loved one would hurt, but I never imagined how much. I cannot imagine losing a marriage partner or a child. Nobody can without experiencing it themselves. Sometimes people remark that we can still talk to Mom, that she can hear us. I personally don't believe that because if she would know our happiness, she'd know our sorrows. I don't think anyone could rest in peace knowing what goes on in this earth. Yes, I long for her to know some things, but then I hope she has so much better than what we can offer her.

I'm still trying to wrap up the sewing before the gardening and cleaning for church starts. How I look forward to that! The other day I heard the little ones talking about going barefoot again, and they got all excited! It made my heart thump a little faster too! In the summertime my *Nothinz** and I are partners from morning until night.

I like the movement of doing more with less. It's no secret what shape the economy is in. It puts a challenge on us keepers at home to see if we can take it to one more level. We can encourage one another and help each other find more ways to be sufficient with what we can raise and make on our own. I often ask myself, do we really need this? How I struggle with this. It's definitely not easy, but I keep praying to come to grips with what we have and be totally satisfied. We live in a materialized world, and temptations are around us daily. I also believe that as professing to be Plain people, we have an advantage of being taught to be keepers at home, to sew, to plant, to reap, and to preserve. I still have so much to learn! I am thankful to be surrounded by Christian women who so willingly teach by example, living their lives to glorify the Lord.

I'm wanting to sit down to do some writing. I've searched through Wayne's desk, through my drawers, and finally through the little girls' treasure drawers until I finally found a tablet with a couple clean sheets of paper. With five writing females plus a son who loves to draw living in this house, I believe I must start buying paper by the case. I did find some other treasures during the search. It's time I cleaned out their treasure drawers while they're either asleep or outside. But they do have so much fun with their treasures and imaginations.

Yesterday we had fun too. After lunch I stirred together a batch of raised donuts. The batch calls for 16 cups of flour, so it makes around 80 big donuts. I laid down with Jolisa and Jesse so they'd quickly fall asleep while the dough was rising. Pretty soon Emily came to tell me the "Thatsa" bowl lid is pushed way up already. I could easily have snoozed a while longer, but I envisioned a dough mess on top of the refrigerator. That gave me strength to get my lazy body moving again.

While I cut circles with an empty tin can, Emily cut the inner circles with a donut cutter. We both had a blast. By that time the oil was hot, so I started frying the first ones. In the meantime, I dumped powdered sugar, Karo, vanilla, and water into a bowl. Emily stirred the frosting together. By then Wayne was in the house to stick his nose into the operation and to taste-test the first of the finished product. Emily ran upstairs to fetch an extra curtain rod, and Wayne stuck one end into a top worktable drawer so it extended out about three-and-a-half feet. Emily put wax paper on the floor beneath it to catch the dripping frosting. Thus we hung the donuts on the curtain rods to drip! That's what you call country boy ingenuity!

By then Jolisa was awake and totally willing to help do whatever she could. Once I was done frying, we finished dipping the donuts in a hurry. Emily and Jolisa had a blast catching frosting with little bowls and scraping it back into the big bowl. About then Jesse woke up from his nap. The look on his face was pure delight.

We cleaned up the floor after we were done, but for some reason it was still sticky there this morning. I was glad it was cleaning day today. We had a lot of fun, and I had to think of my Grandma Raber and how I used to help her make donuts. I hope my girls will someday think back to our sticky donut-making days.

Contrary to popular belief, we do not need to leave the comfort of our own homes to make some wonderful childhood memories. These sweet, calorie-loaded circles of dough sure don't last long, but I want to remember the declarations of joy I heard from my family and the other families we shared with and how they helped me know my time and efforts were well appreciated. My time spells love to them. What else am I here for?

◇◇◇◇◇

What is sweeter than your child getting up from a nap and just being lazy for a while? Scratching his cheeks and then his knee. Yawning once, then twice—the second time really loudly. Big brown eyes watching me, and then the boy grinning lazily when our eyes meet. I asked him if he wanted to be held a while, but today he refuses. Now he wants a drink and help with his clothes to go outside. He's growing so fast!

My thoughts go back to those days when we first brought him home from the hospital. I remember the episode when we gave him his first bath. The three little girls wanted to be in the bathroom with us, one holding the soap, one holding the lotion, and the other the towel. It didn't go too well because Jolisa couldn't handle his "ouchy belly." Then, as is so common for little boys, Jesse peed high into the air, causing more screeches from his sisters. For the first year and a half he was so fussy, but now he is such a happy little fellow.

Jesse has a little cousin his age named Jeryl. They are the best of buddies. They remind me of the "You been farming long?" pictures of little boys dressed like adult farmers in coveralls, boots, and hats. These thoughts make me miss Mom because she'd love to watch Jesse and Jeryl in their play.

◇◇◇◇◇

Today is a beautiful Saturday. Wayne is hauling manure, and the children are outside playing. I'm surprised Brian hasn't been in with more dove breasts to fry. He shoots them with his BB gun. Now he's started cutting off the breasts to eat. I haven't gotten the chance to taste any because the children gobbled them right up!

◇◇◇◇◇

With eagerness I'm watching the plants grow that I started indoors. I have three kinds of tomatoes, bell peppers, salsa peppers, geraniums, purple salvias, and mini-marigolds. I'm always eager to dig in the dirt by this time of the year.

I do need to do a bunch of sewing yet though. It's pathetic how little time I get to do it. Seems there is always laundry and baking and— poof!—the week is gone. That dream about making greeting cards to last a year is still just that.

◇◇◇◇◇

Wayne is eager to start haying because our barn is empty of our own. We're praying for a good crop. I'd love to be out helping Wayne with the second shift of milking, but other jobs are calling for my attention. One reason I love to help him with milking is getting fresh air. It helps clear the cobwebs from my brain. I love spending the time with Wayne mostly. Drinking a mug of coffee as we milk. Having quite the conversations. Sometimes we've solved half the world's problems. Sometimes we can't even figure out the minutest problem in our own little world. It's amazing how we don't smell the cow smell when we're helping, but how much it stinks when we're not helping and the workers come in from the barn.

◇◇◇◇◇

We stretch, and yawn, and try to gather our thoughts together...too long after the alarm has gone off. It's Monday morning, and we're lazy from our relaxing, overeating Sunday. We were invited to my Uncle Ervin and Aunt Clara's for lunch, and what a treat that was. They served grilled chicken, mashed potatoes, gravy, and the works. It felt wonderful to be there.

◇◇◇◇◇

School is out! Wayne, Brian, and I went out to chore this morning, and Colleen started with the laundry right away. After breakfast I heated two gallons of milk for making yogurt. Karah and Emily washed a counter-full of dishes. They are lucky our counter isn't big!

I finished sewing some wall-hangings for my sister to sell, and Colleen made some cards. That got the little girls started with stamps, ink, stickers, and brads. What a mess they quickly had. They had fun and cleaned it all up by lunchtime. Before lunch I started making some desserts, doing more steps with the yogurt, and stirring together a double-batch of waffles. By then Colleen was washing dishes again. She also peeled potatoes to fry to go with our waffles and then got out fresh sausage links and fresh maple syrup. Some friends gave us a whole gallon of the syrup! I had to immediately buy some vanilla ice cream and douse it with maple syrup. That was so-o-o-o good but very hard on my diet.

After we ate, I started a batch of bread. I then laid down with Jesse until he was sleeping. That short nap gave me a boost too. Sad to say, but Colleen advised me to rest, hoping I wouldn't be so grouchy and short with the children. How I need the Lord to guide me each day, and oh, how I fall short every day. I'm so glad he's still working on me.

Before lunch it started raining, so the girls all ran for the wash lines and brought in the laundry. Some of it had actually dried, and the rest we hung around the house and under the porch roof. Now Colleen is washing the dishes again, and Karah and Emily are sweeping the house.

Wayne and Brian hauled manure, scraped the barn, and did regular farm necessities. It had just dried off enough that they could get into the fields, and now it is raining again. Looks like we'll have a late-planting season because of all the moisture. With our heavy clay soil, we need to be patient.

Cottage Cheese

I've started making cottage cheese, and most of us really like it. Some of the children wrinkle up their noses, but they don't like store-bought either. I rarely buy some as it is too expensive, but I'm glad others do because it helps the dairy industry.

It's really simple to make. All you need is a gallon of milk (I use raw), one-half cup white vinegar, a bit of salt, sour cream, cream, or whipped topping, whichever you prefer.

You need to heat the milk to 180 degrees. Pour in the vinegar slowly, really stirring it. Turn off the heat. I line a strainer with really thin fabric and then pour the milk (and curds) into the strainer. Wash the curds using cool water, tossing them in the process. I just use my hands to do this. Twist the straining cloth tightly and put something heavy on top of the curds for 15 minutes.

Dump the curds into a bowl, add a little salt to taste, and use a fork to stir. Then I add three or four tablespoons sour cream and enough milk to make the consistency how I like it. If you'd like it fluffier, add some whipped topping. If you think the curds are too hard, the milk probably got too hot.

Jolisa and I love eating the dry, salted curds without the cream or anything.

Year 2

Summer

This is a typical summer evening. I'm having a hard time getting the children inside and into the bathtub. Once they are in the tub, I have a hard time getting them out again and upstairs to bed. We love these beautiful summer days!

It was fun clearing my porch table of all the plants I'd started and moving them outside into the garden area. I learned more things about starting plants from seed, and I look forward to expanding my efforts next year. I only had to buy a couple plants at the greenhouse. That feels like a major accomplishment! My flower beds aren't showcases, but it's fun to see what all I can do with what I have.

Jesse loves being outside from morning till night. He is Brian's shadow, gaining knowledge as fast as his three-year-old mind can comprehend. He has some "smooth moves" when bouncing a basketball. It's cute to watch. It's also surprising how much he notices and imitates. For all he notices, I hope we're making our footsteps plain enough so we're easy to follow. He plays a lot with his buddy, Sam the dog, and spends hours in the sandbox. Today the dairy supply salesman was here, and Jesse said the man had a candy-full box. We would've said a box full of candy. One day Jesse wanted "coffee servers" during church. He kept looking in Wayne's pockets, and Wayne couldn't figure out what he wanted. On the way home we decided he'd wanted Life Savers because a couple weeks earlier Wayne had some.

One day Jesse came in through the washhouse telling me he had washed his stinky shoes. I immediately became alarmed because he can't reach the faucet. I thought of my Sunday whites in soak out in the washroom. You guessed it. My whites had sad spots of horse manure all over them. Luckily I was able to get them clean!

◇◇◇◇◇

I try to walk two miles at least four or five days a week. Oftentimes at least one, if not all three, of the little girls go along. We sometimes have quite the conversations. One day Karah told me her "sold core" hurts so bad. I was spinning "sold core" through my mind. I had to laugh once it soaked in what she meant. She had a painful cold sore. She can do spoonerisms without even trying.

Today I sewed a Triple Irish Chain quilt together. I had strip-pieced the strips together earlier and then cut them apart. Now today I finished it. It took me all day. Colleen did the laundry, baked cookies, and other little whatnots that had to be done. The little girls helped by cleaning up the house and washing dishes. Seems there are always dishes to wash. I do need to get some charts made for the girls to keep things running smoothly. Everybody is concerned they don't do more than their share.

I went on a walk as the girls washed the supper dishes. Then Jesse needed a haircut. Those would only last half as long if I could convince him to sit still. I actually nipped a little skin tonight. Cost a couple tears.

Wayne wanted help with some tax papers, which is total Greek to me. I ended up helping a little. Glad that's ready for the mailman and out of my hair.

My dad was in Oklahoma with my sister Freda and family for three weeks. Now he's coming home tomorrow night. We'll be glad to have him back. Our friends Vern and Sandy from Oklahoma are bringing him home, and Sister Freda is coming along! That's cause for some excitement around here. We quickly planned for the family to gather here. They will only be here for one day and two nights—short but sweet.

◇◇◇◇◇

I can't handle fumes from strong cleaners, but I haven't found a stain remover that's ecofriendly but does a job like the strong cleaners. I use a lot of white vinegar to clean most anything, but some things just need more. Plus, we have hard water so it takes more soap. I add softener salt to the laundry water, and that helps on conserving soap. Adding baking soda to the dishwater helps soften the water, thus it takes less soap.

◇◇◇◇◇

Our sewing is pretty well caught up for now, except for my dress suit I need for a neighbor's wedding. We're all excited for her and looking forward to her wedding day. Then a bit of sadness settles in because we will miss her in the neighborhood. Her husband will take her 11 miles from here to help him milk cows.

Colleen does need a few summer dresses yet, and then we will need to put all sewing to the side. We have to do some serious cleaning. I'm looking forward to that too, but I just wish the cleanliness and orderly closets would last longer.

◇◇◇◇◇

It will again take more time getting the meals on the table once the garden things are in full swing. It takes a while to gather and prepare all the fresh produce, but I'd sure hate to miss it. We have so much to be thankful for. It'll take a lot of bread again so we can fully enjoy those radishes, green onions, and lettuce. We don't have our own strawberries this year, but I started 80-some plants, so next year we hope to have a lot. I am still hoping for a big raspberry crop this year. Dare I?

It's a bit chilly and cloudy today, resulting in the living room looking like a disaster area, the bathroom feels and smells like a swamp, and we're caged inside the house by laundry hanging under the porch roof. Other than that, I'm okay.

The reason for the disastrous living room is because the four little ones are playing dolls. Actually, they are planning how they want to play more than they're actually playing. The dolls' names get changed numerous times. One decides to live in a certain place, and then no, the other decides to live there, and so on and on. My "little" ones are now ages three and a half, five and a half, seven, and eight and a half. Not so little anymore.

Yesterday was an awesome day. For a while there I wondered why we even try to be farmers, but by bedtime I was convinced again. After breakfast Wayne and Brian started raking 10 acres of hay. Colleen and I worked at cleaning out the kitchen cupboards and the pantry. I emptied all the canisters and scrubbed those really well. I rearranged some things, took some to the attic, and threw some out. We enjoyed what we were doing. In the midst of all that, my friend Esther came over with a big bag of asparagus and some other goodies for us. In the morning I'd kept hoping she would drop by. The children all cheered to see the asparagus, which we are now having for lunch today.

Yesterday for lunch Colleen made tacos and warmed up some leftover scalloped potatoes. Wayne and Brian didn't come in from raking until the potatoes were pretty well crisp. We ended up dumping those and fixing the tacos and wrapping them in foil to keep them warm.

I put Jesse down for a nap, hurriedly washed the dishes, and prepared some iced tea for the water jugs. Colleen went on the road to our neighbors' to ask for help in the hay making. Brian and Karah helped me get started with the milking.

Later, Emily swept the kitchen. Karah and I did the milking while the men, including some neighbors, did the haying. Colleen helped the men with the unloading and stacking.

After chores I quickly baked some cookies; collected and refilled water jugs, and took them to the men who were putting up hay. I pulled some weeds in the gardens, planted a Vinca plant, and then mowed the yard. I also ran the weed-eater until it ran out of gas. Emily, Jolisa, Jesse, and I biked over to our freezer at the neighbor's to get meat and some vanilla ice cream.

I then drove the team and hauled wagons of hay from the field. Our baler kept giving the men fits. That's why it took so long. Our neighbor Junior finally went home and got his baler to use. For a while I was afraid we wouldn't get it all into the barn and there was rain in the forecast. That's what's called stress!

Finally at 8:00 I made toasted egg sandwiches with onions and cheese. I wrapped those in foil to keep them warm. Wayne, the boys, and Colleen finally came into the house at 9:00, saying we got over 1100 bales! That's when it feels good to be farmers.

Sitting around the kitchen table, everyone wanted to tell their story. They all wanted to talk at once. We ate vanilla ice cream and fresh strawberries. We took our showers, and the children headed for bed. I decided I needed another one. Earlier, while milking, one of the cows knocked the hose off the wall mount with the nozzle landing on the cement hard enough that water sprayed to the ceiling. I had no choice but to get sopping wet while shutting it off. I really didn't consider that my final shower.

This spring my sister Ida, who lives across the driveway from us, had a lot of volunteer flowers come up in one of her flower beds. One day she and I transplanted a lot of these blue salvias. They grew into beautiful plants but didn't get any buds. They just didn't look quite right. Finally I was convinced these plants were weeds, although the leaves looked very similar to the blue salvias. I quickly got rid of those weeds and replaced them with real flowers. Every once in a while it's good to laugh at ourselves.

◇◇◇◇◇

With the hay in the barn, I'll now start praying for a rainy day as I really need my hubby in the house for a couple hours. Probably a month ago already, maybe even a month and a half ago, I tried fixing our cold water faucet in the bathtub because it hadn't been working right for a while. Well, I ended up ruining it, and we've not been able to use it since. It's a good thing Dad's house is attached because we use his shower a lot. For baths we dump in the cold water with a pail. It works, but it's very inconvenient. I will totally appreciate running water once it's working again.

The kitchen sink faucet leaks too. I guess I'll keep my hands off that because I just ruin things. Hmmm, on second thought, that could be a good idea after all. Maybe then it would get fixed. That's just the life of a farmer's wife once the field work is in full swing. We take things for granted when everything works. I sure do.

◇◇◇◇◇

I've been eating yogurt topped with granola for breakfast for the last several weeks. My friend Esther gave me a baggie of granola she'd made. I'd wanted to try it because I'd never had some that I really liked. Well, this is delicious! Now I could eat yogurt and granola three meals a day. I like to slice a banana into my bowl first, then add yogurt, and put the granola on top.

I baked a batch of bread today. It seems I have to do that every four or five days. I love fresh bread with Miracle Whip, fresh garden lettuce, and just-picked green onions. Next to ripen that's good for summer sandwiches is yellow summer squash.

◇◇◇◇◇

We're enjoying our hummingbirds again. We have a feeder hanging outside the kitchen window. It doesn't take them long to get used to all the comings and goings through our kitchen door. We can get pretty close to them. They are amazing little creatures.

◇◇◇◇◇

Why does our bathroom remind me of a swamp on a damp day? Well, it's exceedingly small and dark with no outside window to open for fresh air. With eight people using it frequently, it just gets that way. Once it really warms up outside, I'll open the small window above the tub. It opens into our washhouse. That really helps. It's an old crank window that takes two of us to open. One pulls from the outside and one uses pliers on the crank and pushes from the inside. That's why we wait to open it until it stays warm—if it cools off outside, we suffer in the tub. Hopefully better days are ahead! We really do have a cozy house that I enjoy. It has a lot of character, as older homes do. Remodeled here and there and waiting for more.

◇◇◇◇◇

You should see my hands. If I modeled them, they'd be the ones beside the perfect ones and labeled "before." They are all scratched, purple and black, fingernails broken and uneven. But that's fine with me—our house is clean! My hands have done a lot of cleaning and scrubbing lately, plus picking and cleaning peas and green beans, pulling weeds, and all that fun stuff. The scratches and purple stains came from picking black raspberries and turning them into pie filling.

For the last two weeks I've been hearing ladies tell their big stories of bounteous black raspberry pickings here and there. They were picking 25 quarts and more at a time. I was becoming very green with jealousy. My patch in the east garden did better than last year, but not great. Brian and I went back to our woods and picked maybe three sandwich baggies full. We were knee-deep in cleaning for church service at our house, so I didn't have time to venture any further. We also had green beans and peas that had to be done.

We got ready for church okay...or actually we just called it quits again and went. There's always more that could be done around here, but there comes a time to sigh and be satisfied.

We are dry. Everything was so dusty, plus we thought we should have spent the time to water the gardens and flower beds. Then on Saturday morning, after chores, we had a beautiful shower of rain. I really didn't mind the splattered windows because I was so thankful for the moisture. It settled the dust and gave the plants a needed boost.

We had surprise visitors in church, which pleased us. It was a beautiful day to host services in our big garage. My brother Jay and his family stayed for a supper of grilled hamburgers and ice cream. Made me lonely for Mom. Time has a way of swiftly moving on.

Jesse played so hard with his buddy Jeryl all afternoon and evening. He could hardly control himself anymore by evening. We all went to bed with the sun still shining brightly.

Monday morning Colleen did a huge laundry. We cleaned up the shop where services were held, and the little girls swept the house. I picked two rows of green beans and ended up selling those as I've already canned all we need. The plants keep producing nice beans, and I have a hard time pulling out plants even if we don't need them. Beans are so good to eat fresh, so I'll keep the plants a while longer.

Colleen brought in red potatoes, yellow summer squash, and

cucumbers for lunch. Nothing beats the taste of fresh, homegrown, by-the-sweat-of-your-brow garden vegetables.

In the forenoon, we received a voice mail message from my sister-in-law. She wondered if we'd like to come pick black raspberries. She and her daughter had gone back to the woods in the morning, and there were still a lot there. Oh, did we ever want to go!

I called back that we'd come down in the evening. We hurried through chores and ate our supper of bologna, lettuce, and cheese sandwiches and pretzels on the hour-long drive with the horse and buggy to their farm. Once we got there, we walked a half mile back to the woods. The four little ones stayed up by the buildings to play with their little cousins. That was a good arrangement for us all. We ended up with four adults and five older children back in the woods. It was fun, peaceful, giggly, scratchy, and beautiful. I was overflowing with thankfulness for the opportunity of picking black raspberries. The berries were the tail-end of the season and a bit smaller, but I didn't mind. We had raspberries!

◇◇◇◇◇

This forenoon I processed the black raspberries into pie filling—filling 21 quarts! I still have some in the freezer to make jelly with. My sister-in-law Laura gave me those out of the goodness of her heart. She brought them along on Sunday and stuck them in the freezer. I felt humbled for the time she'd spent in picking these and her thoughtfulness.

Next week I want to go pick blueberries for fresh eating and pie filling to can. Fresh blueberry pie is so good. Maybe I should up my daily walking to three miles instead of just two because of the extra sweets.

Talking about pie filling—I also want to can apple pie filling later this fall. I hope to have 60 to 70 quarts of various fillings in the basement for next year. These are so handy for pies, desserts, and Long Johns for my farm family.

I'd like to share my favorite apple pie filling. It looks as beautiful in the jars as it tastes in pie and apple crisp. A quart also makes a nice little gift for someone. I like to tie a pretty ribbon around the lid to fancy it up a bit.

Apple Pie Filling

In an eight-quart kettle, heat to boiling 7 cups water, 5 cups white sugar, and 1 cup brown sugar.

In the meantime, mix 6 tablespoons Perma-flo (or thickener of your choice) with a bit of cold water.

Pour Permo-flo mixture into the sugar water. Stir until thick and smooth. (Sometimes I need to add a bit more Perma-flo to get the consistency I prefer.)

Once mixture is thickened, add 9 cups diced tart apples and 1 teaspoon cinnamon.

Remove mixture from heat and ladle into quart jars (approximately 14), leaving one-inch headspace. Process using water-bath canning for 25 minutes.

◇◇◇◇◇

I really should have planted butternut squash to mix with pumpkins to can for cookies, whoopee pies, and pumpkin pies, but I didn't think about it until it was too late. I even had space in the garden. I like butternut squash and pumpkin mixed together because it has a milder flavor than pure pumpkin.

◇◇◇◇◇

This year has been a good year for roses, with the weather being so cool. They've been putting on quite the show for us. Our rosebushes are outside the kitchen window where I can enjoy them when I'm by the sink. Each time I leave the house I walk past them. Roses are such wondrous gifts from our Lord. To smell and look at one always softens my heart.

◇◇◇◇◇

Sam the dog is enjoying his summer with our children. He loves to play ball with anyone who will take the time to throw it. He plays with Jesse a lot. They are clearly devoted friends. Jesse spends chore time in the barn with Wayne and me. He stays in the milking parlor watching us, sleeping, and drinking milk. I love seeing him and the little girls playing, bottle-feeding the calves, or just watching us milk the cows.

We went back down to twice-a-day milking. Wayne thinks it's crazy because we can't afford to at all, but enough was enough. I love our schedule again but dread the fact that someday soon we'll need to make some changes again. We desperately need higher milk prices or our doors being opened to some other ventures. Maybe not carrying all our eggs in one basket. Even though our main business goal is dairy, we do want to be open-minded.

I hear the vacuum pump purring, so I'd better head for the barn. I don't want to miss out on all the fun.

◇◇◇◇◇

This absolutely beautiful summer is speeding into fall way too fast. I wish I could stomp on the brakes. I feel like flying into a temper tantrum, but I know how much that would help. Fall is beautiful too, but oh how I love summer. My favorite season has to be the shortest one, of course. This summer was so unseasonably cool I barely got a suntan. Most years I tried to do the gardening early morning or later in the evening to avoid the heat, but this year I could do it whenever it suited me because the weather was downright pleasant. We had wonderfully cool nights to snuggle under the covers. I've only twice gone out to chore in the morning without a sweatshirt.

Fall

Our corn crop really feels the milder weather. It wouldn't win a beauty contest if it were the only contestant. It was so wet this spring to begin with, and then it stayed so cool. The corn does look better now that it's closer to harvest time. Corn needs warmer temperatures to fully mature.

The sweet corn in the garden did great. We froze 96 quarts and ate corn-on-the-cob until we felt like hogs. Emily's front teeth allowed her to enjoy it this year. She'd been teased quite a bit because it appeared for a while she might be missing her upper front teeth through corn season. One new one grew in time, and one old one is still hanging on.

For some reason I didn't mind the mess of eating corn so much this year. I guess the children are all a year older so most of the corn went into their mouths instead of onto the floor.

Colleen finished her schooling, and having her home from school is wonderful! She thinks so too. This term Brian is in the seventh grade; Karah a third grader; and Emily is in the first grade. Jolisa and Jesse play nicely together here at home. We always have a period of adjusting once school starts in the fall, but there are things I like about it too. The 8:15 bedtime for the children is nice. It gives me a little quiet time to read—if I don't fall asleep. Emily has been a borderline reader for a while already, and I am really looking forward to her learning to fully read anything she wants. We all love books, and it's always a thrill when each child masters reading fluently.

Before I forget to mention it, we're back to milking three times a day. I kicked, and screamed, and banged my head—all to no avail. Not really. No, I absolutely didn't want to, but I realized we had to. Therefore I prayed for peace, which I was granted. Wayne read in a dairy magazine how the dairy *food* producers had over 100 percent greater profits the first half of this year over the first half of last year. Well, of course, with not more than they're paying for the milk, they can fill their pockets with more profits. It angers me that the middleman makes more than the farmer does, but what can a little Amish woman do about it?

I've acquired a couple new recipes to try—sour cream, cream cheese, soft cheese, mozzarella, and hard cheese. I've already made the mozzarella, and that is exactly what it tastes like. I was amazed. I feel privileged to have raw, whole milk at my fingertips to experiment with such foods, giving me a whole new appreciation for these products. I haven't tried the other recipes yet, but I will as my schedule allows.

We love cheese, especially with homemade bologna and crackers. Cheese has a way of putting a finishing touch on almost any dish, any soup, any sandwich.

I definitely need to start walking three miles a day.

Our good friends Vernon, Sandy, Jeff, and Connie from Oklahoma spent three days in the area. We were privileged to make precious memories with them again. They brought some lavender scents that I'd been looking for to add to my homemade fabric softener.

Fabric Softener

Stir together 2 cups white vinegar, 2 cups baking soda, and 4 cups water. Sometimes I add ½-cup hair conditioner.

Mix it together in a plenty big container as it will really foam when you stir the vinegar and soda together.

Store in empty fabric softener bottles. Shake well before using. Use ¼-cup per wash load.

There is a first time for everything. Tonight for the first time I experienced the thrill(?) of cleaning fish that Brian caught today. A neighbor man took Brian fishing, and he had an awesome day catching a lot of fish. We look forward to having a fish-fry tomorrow night.

I'm remembering the week of the Fourth of July because it was downright chilly like today. It put a lot of campers into long johns. One 50-degree morning a grandpa in his sixties was trying to sleep with a thick coat and cap on while wrapped in a thick blanket. His sweet wife Edna, entered the tent, and he told her, "Oh, Grandma, this is so fun, why don't we do it more often?" Grandma laughed so hard she had nearly everyone awake at five o'clock that morning. I loved the grandpa's attitude and cheerfulness; I long to be more like him.

Last night I discovered my alarm-clock battery was dead. I almost never hear Wayne's alarm, and yes, we need two to get us out of bed in the morning. I reminded Wayne that he needs to wake me when his alarm goes off so he doesn't shut his off and fall back to sleep. Well, that is exactly what happened. All at once Wayne woke me up, and it wasn't the time we'd planned to get up. Disgusting! So our day started a half hour later then we'd planned. Chores went as usual...nothing really exciting. Just the right amount of exercise to get my blood flowing for the day.

Colleen spent the night at Aunt Sue's to visit with her cousins, so I knew what all waited for me once I got to the housework. That was okay. I'm spoiled, and the little girls can chip in and do more if they know they have to. While heading toward the house, I grabbed a five-gallon bucket. In the darkness I shoved tomatoes into it. I'd harvested the tomatoes last week already and put them on a board to speed up their ripening. I headed to the house, got myself cleaned up, and then woke the girls. It took quite a bit of coaxing to get them moving.

Karah swept the house. Emily thought she could just go back to bed. I can't remember if she got anything accomplished or not. I do think she cleared the table after breakfast. She loves first grade, but she's not good at handling changes—and school has been a major change for her.

In the meantime, I washed the tomatoes and got them into the pots to cook. I fixed the schoolchildren's lunches and made oatmeal for breakfast. We all gathered in the living room before breakfast to send our praise and thankfulness heavenward. Then we were all aflutter again. I combed the girls' hair, and they finished getting ready for school.

After they headed out, I grabbed the five-gallon bucket again and ran for the garden to get the rest of the ripe tomatoes. It was a beautiful morning, and I listened to the chatter of the neighborhood girls as they biked past on their way to school. Then all was quiet again.

I keep thinking of a year ago today...the day Mom died. Many, many thoughts tumble through my mind. How we all miss her, and that's okay. I rest in the thought that this was the will of God, but I still miss her. The last month has been especially hard.

I have to stay on my toes as my sisters Leanna and Sue and I are going to my Aunt Ida's for lunch today. (She's Mom's sister.) Ida's two daughters, Edna and Erma, will also be there. It will feel good to see everyone. I fixed a bowl of coleslaw to take along for lunch.

Jesse and Jolisa entertained themselves by making a brown cracker and granola mess. They asked umpteen times when we will be ready to go to Aunt Ida's. Poor things. I'm not used to having a schedule like this, and it makes me jumpy. Tomorrow I go away for the day too.

I set up the Victorio strainer and put the cooked tomatoes through for juice. I heated the can lids and lined the quart cans up. I added 2 tablespoons lemon juice (½ teaspoon citric acid or 4 tablespoons regular white vinegar also works) to each can, poured in the tomato juice, slapped the lids on top and screwed on the rings tightly. I waterbath canned them for 35 minutes, took them out, and set them on a towel to seal. *Groan.* Now comes the fun part—cleaning up the mess. It didn't take long because I was on a mission.

Jesse and Jolisa were still asking me when I would be ready to go to Aunt Ida's. We finally went and enjoyed every minute we were there. The meal Aunt Ida prepared was so like what Mom would make when we came home for the day. It warmed us all the way to our hearts. And the stories! It was just so good to be there.

Colleen came home with us, and we are all glad to have her at home again even if she was only gone for a night. She deserved a fun little break with her cousins. We got home at 2:30, and I decided to see if our couch was still comfortable! Stretching out felt wonderful, and I decided not to feel one bit guilty. When the schoolchildren came home they wondered if I was sick.

While the rest of us chored and the little ones played, Colleen washed the tomato juice cans and carried them to the basement. She said there are more than 70 quarts down there now. As long as the plants keep producing, I'll keep canning. We eat a lot of chili soup and tomato gravy in the winter. Wayne would drink more tomato juice if I had a habit of keeping some in the refrigerator. I know that would be good for me too, but ugh and gross. Maybe once I grow up I'll like it too.

◇◇◇◇◇

We had spaghetti and meatballs, along with tomato sandwiches, for supper. Colleen got the campfire roaring to have roasted marshmallows and s'mores for dessert. It seems the summer was so cool and short that we didn't get a lot of s'mores made. I sure ate my share tonight. The house is quiet with the children now in bed. Wayne is reading in his dilapidated recliner. It's time to call it a day. Oh, but I do have to tell you what happened on a Monday back in August.

To begin with, the week after my mom died I discovered I had a secret pal. The first day I was home alone with the little ones, a floral shop delivered a teacup and saucer with a fresh flower arrangement. I was humbled and in awe. It felt like the Lord was telling me he's right here with me. And on it went. Every month I received a gift. In July there was a note attached to the gift saying to be ready on August 31. I had no clue as to who this secret person was.

I decided to piece a scrap log-cabin quilt using leftover fabric from Mom's quilt business to give this person as a gift of appreciation. I had a lot of emotions tied into this quilt because this secret person was really blessing me. So often it seemed I received those gifts just when I needed a lift. Often it felt like the Lord was showing me that he cares for me. I was a bundle of excited nerves by the time August 31 rolled around.

I found out that five ladies from a church district decided to have secret pals for a year. As soon as I saw these ladies, I knew my cousin Edna was my secret pal! She has a quilt business like Mom used to have, so she already has plenty of quilts, but she was still appreciative of the one I'd made for her because of the fabric I used and the emotions involved.

◇◇◇◇◇

Our house is cold on this dreary, rainy day. It seems the last dozen or so times Colleen did laundry it ended up being rainy. Wayne is now trying to get the coal stove started here in the kitchen so we can start unthawing our tight shoulders and maybe think about drying some laundry in here. There really is nothing cozier then a warm fire glowing in one corner of the kitchen. It warms a person to the bones and looks so peaceful.

This morning while I was kneading bread at the kitchen table, Jesse crawled up on the table and started playing in the flour canister. I told him to stop and, of course, he wasn't impressed. He told me I could just go to Shipshewana or Topeka and buy our bread instead of making it. He figured then he wouldn't be tempted to play in the flour.

We've definitely had an abundance of moisture and cool temperatures this year. I didn't get my fill of warm sunshine. I cringe to think of the cold winter months ahead when I can hardly move to do chores because of my many layers of clothing. If you've never had the chance to experience the joys of January and February dairy farming amid frozen water pipes, frozen toes, frozen dresses, and a very cold milking parlor with six or eight cats vying for the milk dish, remember to thank the Lord while you're inside your cozy, warm house looking outside. I'm really thankful, though, that I have a chance to go outside and get fresh air and exercise—even if I sometimes feel like kicking the pesky cats.

One night while Wayne and I were milking, Jesse came to the parlor extremely upset. He was crying hysterically and his knees were shaking against each other. He was repeatedly saying, "The tractor is out!" Brian had been driving the garden tractor, so Wayne figured Jesse was denied a ride and upset about it. With Jesse's carrying on, we decided it might be something more serious than that. I flew up from the parlor (we have four steps from the pit) and into the milk house, afraid of what I would encounter. Wayne was right behind me.

Immediately I saw why Jesse was so upset. The big 4010 John Deere tractor had broken one of the milk house windows! Wayne had left the *commodity shed* * door open in the east end of the barn. Jesse had evidently climbed onto the tractor and was playing. He pulled it out of park, and the tractor proceeded to roll east toward the milk house. The cement is in enough of a downgrade and the tractor, with the

TMR mixer wagon attached to it, was heavy enough that the machinery gained quite a bit of speed. Jesse nipped a 100-gallon gas tank and crashed into a portable basketball hoop, which slammed into the milk house window, thus breaking it. That was the least of my concerns right then. We were shaken, and very thankful that Jesse was unharmed. As I held and comforted Jesse, it seemed I could feel his guardian angel's wings fluttering around us and rejoicing at Jesse's safety with us. It took Jesse a long time to calm down, and he advised Wayne to keep the barn door closed. We all agreed. I cringe to think of the damage that could have been done had the tractor hit the glazed tile blocks of the milk house.

◇◇◇◇◇

Every week I think, *Now this Saturday I want to keep the day more relaxed.* But every week it seems to be just as hectic. By the time we get the cleaning done, maybe bake a bit, and fix other food, the day is jam-packed. We did have a stress buster the other Saturday though.

We were done with the regular weekly cleaning, and Colleen was working by the kitchen cabinets when she heard some peculiar sounds. "Mom, I hear a mouse in here!" she said.

We listened and, yes, we heard that dreaded sound. It seemed to be in distress, and in our kind-hearted way, we wanted to terminate its distress. Colleen and I both went to get brooms. By then Karah, Emily, Jolisa, and Jesse were dancing nervously around the kitchen. We told them to be quiet, and I opened a cupboard and spun the lazy Susan around a couple times to see what would happen.

Colleen and I are typical females, and we had a bad case of the jitters dancing up and down our spines. Probably me more than Colleen because she's usually calmer than I am.

Yeeeiiii! Whop! Whop! Wham! We were dancing around by then because the mouse was on the loose! The noise level was astronomical as we chased the mouse through the kitchen. Above all the noise I screamed to the girls to close the pantry door. We didn't need a mouse in the pantry. The creature ran for the porch as we continued to whop at it. Finally Colleen made a killing hit, and we straightened our backs and sighed. I glanced toward the kitchen and started whooping and laughing because Karah, Emily, Jolisa, and Jesse were all standing on the kitchen table facing us, their eyes wide. Amid our giggling, Colleen said her broom handle was crooked and would never be the same. All these joys of living in an old house. We very rarely do have mice in the house, thankfully.

Another challenge of living in an old house is having cold floors. The older I get, the colder I get. We put a rug in the living room this fall, so it's cozier. Can you tell me anything cozier than enjoying an evening at home with the family relaxing in the living room, munching on popcorn, and reading together? Then, being children, they romp around the rug. Next they might fix a nest with blankets, pillows, and a pile of books. Or perhaps they just talk and giggle. The gas lamplight adds to the warmth, and the quiet hum sounds cozy too. All too soon it's bedtime.

The cows are probably wondering if someone will come out to the barn and milk them tonight. It's chore time, and the way it sounds in here it's high time several of us headed to the barn.

Year 3

Winter

"This is the day which the LORD has made; we will rejoice and be glad in it." It's easy to contemplate Psalm 118:24 on such a beautiful, sunshine-filled day as today. We are to rejoice and be glad on the dreary days too, but it doesn't come so easily then.

I'm aching to head outside and walk two miles, breathing in the fresh air and drinking in the beauty around me. I'd enjoy some quiet time by myself and feeling my muscles working to rid my body of all the sugar and flour I devoured today. I simply disgust myself at times. My self-control went south this morning for some reason. Now I don't even feel good.

I baked a fresh batch of bread this forenoon, so decided to make one loaf of cheddar ranch as a treat for my family. I ate a piece of that for lunch. I also made Rice Crispy Treats for the children, and I had to lick what was stuck on my fingers when I transferred the mixture from the kettle to the pan. Wayne ordered an apple pie, but I haven't tasted those except for a bite of crust that chipped off. For several weeks now I've been aching for a piece of baked cream pie, so on this mighty day of baking I decided to bake three of those. I have no intention of eating them alone. In fact, I'll share with the neighbors.

For the baked cream pie I use my Aunt Barbara's recipe that is deliciously smooth and creamy. My sister Freda knows the recipe by heart. My sisters Ida and Leanna make it a lot. My sister Sue used it for one of her daughter's wedding meals. My married nieces can bake them to perfection. So you see, it is definitely a family favorite. Self-discipline needs to come home again and stay settled.

Cream Pie

1 cup whole cream
2 cups half & half
3 egg whites
½ cup white sugar
1 cup brown sugar
1 rounded Tbsp. flour
Dash of salt (important!)
A little vanilla

Heat cream and half & half to a *slight* scald. Do not boil!

Beat egg whites until frothy. Add white sugar and beat a bit more. Add brown sugar, flour, salt, and vanilla. Mix. Add cream mixture.

Mix and pour into a pastry-lined 9-inch pie pan.

Bake at 400 degrees on bottom shelf until set. (You may need to reduce the temperature because a boiled pie is ruined.)

Wayne, Colleen, and I went on a little excursion for two days—a welcome break in the day-to-day monotony. We went to Daviess County in Southern Indiana. Karah stayed at her classmate Eva's house, Emily stayed at her classmate Alyssa's house, Jolisa and Jesse stayed with my brother Jay's family. Brian got the worst end of the deal because he had to stay home to do the chores. He did get a treat by spending the night at neighbor David's, who helped him with the chores.

We bumped to Daviess County in the backseat of a 15-passenger van that was pulling an enclosed cargo trailer. We had a lot of fun with our fellow passengers. We saw fields of corn and beans, and then more fields of beans and corn. Some scenery we wished we wouldn't have seen because we didn't always know exactly where we were going. We did get there safe and sound...an hour later than anticipated. That small inconvenience was quickly forgotten because of what a good time we had.

The Daviess County Amish know the true meaning of hospitality—i's dotted and t's crossed. We met many people, immensely enjoyed catching up with news from friends and, as always on an outing like that, didn't have enough time to take everything in.

We picked up Jolisa and Jesse on our way home. Jesse was becoming quite concerned about the whereabouts of his mom and daddy. He enjoyed his stay, but two days away from us was long enough, he decided. The rest of the children were at home and waiting for us.

Our school seems to be back on track again after having many sick children. School was closed for three days, which seemed to help a lot. Our three scholars each had the flu, but the rest of us have been fortunate so far.

Wayne came in at noon and said we have a *fresh heifer*,* which is good news for the *bulk tank*.* However, the calf pen population remains the same because the calf didn't survive. Hopefully we won't have a rodeo when we milk tonight. The heifer seems to be kind of wild. You all know how I love to chase heifers.

We're back to milking twice a day. Wayne explains it thus: A candle can burn for so long, and then the fire burns out. We did it for a year and a half and finally burned out. The milk price seems to be steadily climbing, but it will take a long, long time to rebound.

Lord willing, we are scheduled to host church services in January, which will be a new experience for us. We usually host in the summer months when we can use the shop building. Our church is smaller now because we divided into two districts to better accommodate people in our homes. We plan to host in our house. In our community, our house is classified as small, but there was a lady here from Texas one time who exclaimed our house was *huge*. So it all depends on what a person is used to. We'll move all our furniture out of the house and set up wooden benches to accommodate everyone. Hosting church services are a privilege that I long never to take for granted. It's a precious experience.

◇◇◇◇◇

Bah humbug! Oh no, no, no, no! I shouldn't feel that way. For this is the day that the Lord made. I do sincerely want to rejoice and be glad in it. It's just so very dreary, foggy, muddy, slippery, and slimy. I force myself to dream of summertime. Now there is a thought. Maybe if I could bring sunshine into someone else's life the sun will shine for me again too. Since we are in February, maybe I can get out some pretty paper and make some valentines!

I hope the people around me know I love them. I know how it brightens up my day when people make an effort to let me know they love me, even with something as simple as a piece of scrap paper with a couple hearts drawn on it. People, especially ladies, like to be told they are loved. I most certainly feel loved without being told all the time because actions speak louder than words, but no one can deny the power of a love note. It doesn't matter if it's between husband and wife, parents and children, friend and friend—whoever it may be, a love note is wonderful.

Recently I received a very descriptive poem about bottle-feeding a calf. As silly as it was, it made my day. We have four bottle-fed calves at this time, so it's very fresh in my mind. The note also reminded me that I'm not the only woman out there in the cold getting slobbered over by these mannerless little creatures. I'm very thankful for these healthy calves, but when I'm trying to train a calf to drink and she acts so totally uncivilized, I do start to feel very lonely. Once these calves get used to it, I do enjoy feeding them. We have a little miracle calf in the barn right now. She did not—or could not—drink from a bottle for a couple days. Wayne kept working with her and shoving white fossil flour down her throat. Lo and behold, she finally started taking an interest in life.

We have three calves in the same pen, and they all want to be fed first. Plus they want the second and third bottles too. On these cold days, it actually feels good to stick my frozen fingers into the mouths that aren't being fed. It helps thaw them out. Now don't get grossed out. I always wear latex gloves to do chores.

This winter I'm in the barn about two-and-a-half hours at a time, sometimes more. As long as we can stay at milking twice a day, I love it. Sometimes ladies tell me hopefully that someday I can stay inside and my children can do my share of the chores. Maybe I'm being selfish, but I really have no desire of graduating to that state. Taking off once in a while is possible now, and I do enjoy that. But I wonder how I'd keep my sanity if I couldn't escape out to the barn—especially in the wintertime. Well, when I get up in the morning and hear the icy north wind howling and the snow is blowing, I do have my weaker moments.

For supper these cold, winter evenings, we're eating soup...and more soup. Tonight we're having homemade mushroom soup. Colleen is our evening cook.

Homemade Mushroom Soup

Sauté fresh, chopped button mushrooms and onions in butter. Colleen uses 1 small box of the mushrooms, about ½-cup of onions, and 2 tablespoons of butter.

Mix 12 tablespoons of flour and some chicken broth, stirring it until smooth.

Add 48 ounces of chicken broth and cook until slightly thickened.

Add 2 cups of cream and simmer for 15 minutes. Add salt and pepper to suit your tastes.

The chicken broth we have canned in the basement has chicken bits in it, so I buy plain broth at our local, bulk-food store. I've made the soup with the chicken bits in it, and it's good too, but we prefer using the plain broth. It's good and creamy using whole milk instead of the cream, which is easier on calorie intake.

I've said before how I'm not that good of a cinnamon roll baker. Well, I've found a way I can doctor them up so they are delicious! I bake the cinnamon rolls as usual. Once they're cooled just slightly, I squeeze a mixture of 4-ounces cream cheese, one 3.5-ounce box instant vanilla pudding, and enough milk to get the right spreading consistency into the circles. You have to gently push the circles apart just a tad. Then frost them with a caramel frosting. These are not too friendly on the calories.

I tried a new honey oatmeal bread recipe lately. Once I had it kneaded and ready to rise for the first time, I discovered I'd forgotten to add the yeast! I'd had too many things going at one time and lost my brain somewhere along the line. I quickly mixed the yeast and water, dumped it into the bowl, and kneaded the bread dough some more. It turned out fine. In fact, it turned out pretty good!

One day at a quilting bee with my aunts and cousins, the art of baking bread was dissected from one end to the next. Interesting. Some roll it out and don't prick the tops. Some shape it with their hands and prick the tops with a fork to eliminate any air bubbles. Some brush the freshly baked loaves with butter; some absolutely don't. Oven temps and length of baking varied. We all thought our own was perfectly good! We enjoy baking our own bread. It makes me feel like a woman and a "keeper at home." Fresh loaves of bread are love notes to my husband and children.

At one of our Raber Christmas gatherings, the adults all had envelopes under their plates that were very mysterious. We were forbidden to open them until we'd finished eating our meal. Dad was then instructed to open his and do whatever he was bidden to do. His envelope contained a poem that he was to stand up and read to the rest of us. So on down the line it went. My uncles and aunts went after Dad. Some read stories. Some led songs that we all pitched in and helped sing. Some read humorous articles. Some shared memories of loved ones gone on before us. We laughed, we sang, we cried. Those memories make me cry. It was a very special time spent with loved ones and worth a whole lot more than playing games and not really sharing our feelings—especially if we have an intense desire to spend time once more with loved ones gone before us.

I'm once again thinking of starting my flower and vegetable seeds in the house. There is hope that spring will be on the way. My flower beds look quite haggard this winter, but I decided not to be intimidated by the perfectly manicured flower beds of neighboring farms and leave some of my annuals out to reseed themselves for the next growing season.

I saw by the looks of the onions in the crates in the basement that we'd better start eating onion rings, fried onions, and, once we butcher, liver and onions to get those crates empty. We do all love onions. Jesse eats them raw with any meal. We had a good crop last year, and I hate to see them spoil. Maybe I'll give some away...with a love note and mouth rinse or breath mints.

Year 3

Spring

This is a diary of a week while we were preparing to host church services in our home.

Monday. This morning while Wayne, Brian, and I did the chores, Colleen cleaned up the house and made tomato gravy and fresh bran muffins for breakfast. Once I got into the house and cleaned myself up, I helped Karah and Emily pack their lunches for school. I made fried-egg sandwiches, and they added tortilla chips and salsa. Brian also wanted a muffin in his lunch. For breakfast, Emily ate cereal, I had my normal yogurt and granola, and the rest ate tomato gravy over soda crackers and bran muffins.

Colleen did the mundane chore of the Monday-morning laundry while I baked a batch of granola, washed a huge amount of dirty dishes, and accomplished other odds and ends that needed to be done on a Monday morning.

Dad is leaving for vacation in Florida soon, so we spent some time with him. Jesse will surely miss his grandpa. It's almost uncanny how Jesse and his grandpa are look-alikes.

I cleaned two refrigerators and Dad's oven. These are not some of my favorite jobs, so I'm always glad when they can be crossed off my list. Colleen washed off the upstairs hallway walls and ceilings, cleaned out the chore-clothes closet, and straightened the cereal shelves in the kitchen cabinets. We warmed up leftovers for lunch. Wayne was readying the shop for butchering tomorrow. Yes, we'll have church here in 13 days, but we have a downed fresh heifer we need to butcher. We've been out of hamburger for a while already, so in no way do I want to pass up this meat. To me, it's not any different than when we have church in the busy summertime hay-making season.

We baked a batch of apple crisp to take along to the monthly neighborhood gathering tonight. I also stirred a batch of black raspberry rolls together for tomorrow.

Tuesday. At 8:05 PM I'm relaxing in front of the cozy coal stove. Jesse's nose is about two inches from my pen. Now Karah's face is about six inches from my paper. Jesse's amazed at my lines and dots. The children are so much fun. It feels absolutely wonderful to relax my tired legs. We're all at home...a restful evening. Here's how the day went.

After our regular morning routine of doing the chores, breakfast, getting the scholars off to school, the rest of us rushed about to get to the shop as soon as we could to start butchering. I was a little out of routine because I had to get the raspberry rolls into the pans to rise before I could leave the house. They were ready for the oven when I got back to the house about an hour and a half later.

A church friend named Ervin, neighbor Loretta, Sister-in-law Nettie, Wayne, Colleen, and I had the beef ready to grind by noon. What a fun time we had together.

Colleen warmed up leftover lasagna and corn for lunch. Applesauce was our salad. We had raspberry rolls and leftover pie for dessert. Coffee helped us stay warm throughout the day. We're so thankful for the fresh meat in the freezer. No fancy gift could make me happier. We also canned 14 quarts of beef chunks tonight.

By evening I could easily have forgone the chores and relaxed a while, but alas, the chores can't be ignored.

Colleen made fresh liver and onions for supper. With all that extra iron we should have a lot of energy tomorrow. I hope so, because it's high time to clean again.

The girls helped put the butchering supplies away and cleaned up the house. It almost seems like a dream that we butchered today.

Tonight Dad left a message on the phone saying he arrived in Florida this morning, and it was 32 degrees. He was cold. I feel sorry for the Florida farmers. I know what a challenge farming is and how much of our lives depend on the weather. Global warming?

Wednesday. It's morning and chores again. Laundry again. This forenoon I made 15 pounds of summer sausage. It took me a lot longer than I had anticipated, and pretty soon I was becoming impatient. I felt it was time to get moving on cleaning house.

After Colleen was done with our regular laundry, I washed bedding, curtains, throws, doilies, carpets, and so forth. It was a cold and windy day, but beautiful. The first time I went to the lines to hang up the sheets, I noticed some of the towels were hanging by one pin, so I fixed those. Next I hung out a quilt. Soon after that, I hung out the comforter. By that time, the quilt was barely hanging on the lines. I fixed that and then went for more washing. My fingers were fairly frozen by then.

The next time I came out to the lines, one was broken and the laundry was flopping and lying on the snow. Finally, at 11:15, I was done. I went inside and quickly made sloppy Joe sandwiches and noodles for lunch. Colleen had washed a huge amount of dirty dishes and watched the two pressure cookers of beef chunks as they processed.

After lunch, Jesse, Jolisa, and I laid down to take a nap. As soon as they were asleep, I got up again. I needed to discipline Jesse once as he and Jolisa would whisper and giggle until the cows came home.

This afternoon we brought up a couple cans of spoiled food from the basement. We emptied them out and washed the cans. We took those and the beef chunk cans to the basement. Now we can have beef stew for supper again. There were more dishes to wash again this afternoon. Emily washed dishes before supper, and after supper we washed dishes again. Bored? Never!

Before chores, Wayne and I took the hamburger and steaks to the freezer at the neighbor's. I made a dozen slips with jobs written on them for Karah and Emily for their chores after school. That took some of the monotony out of those mundane jobs of putting dishes and laundry away. We had fried hamburgers and smoothies for supper. Wayne popped popcorn after supper. He read a story to the little ones, and then it was time for bed.

Thursday. Chores again this morning. After getting to the house we had the usual filling of lunch pails, sweeping the kitchen, plus I made a double-batch of Rice Crispy squares so we'd have something to put in the lunches. I made several butlers [carafes] of coffee and tea so my two lovely sisters and two lovely sisters-in-law could warm up once they got here after lengthy buggy rides.

We had a good warming up once they arrived. We all live good distances apart and don't get together all that often, so it's good to sit a while and just catch up on each other's lives. Jesse and Jolisa enjoyed playing with their little cousins Kristina, Lora, and Jeryl. We thoroughly cleaned Dad's house, talked, and, of course, ate again at noon.

Colleen washed more curtains and bedding this morning. It was a breezy, beautiful, close to 40-degree day. Perfect for laundry. Supper was beef stew and summer sausage with crackers. We washed the dishes, read to the girls, and now, after showers, the children are in bed. It's my turn! I can hardly wait to feel those clean, crisp sheets on my aching legs. Thank you, Lord, for a special, beautiful day.

Friday. Chores again. Colleen baked a double-batch of monster cookie bars for lunches and snacks. The girls fixed the lunches, and I started two batches of yogurt. Colleen did laundry again. I scrubbed the kitchen floor and gave it a good shining. There are always things to organize and put away, so that's what I did the rest of the forenoon. I'd wanted to get stew out of the refrigerator to warm up for lunch, but when I opened the fridge door to get it, the can of stew dumped on my clean kitchen floor. So what could I do except get paper towels and proceed to clean it up.

Colleen ironed the whites and helped the little ones clean up their toys. I laid down with Jesse until he fell asleep. There are more dishes to wash, and the kitchen needs to be swept again because the children enjoyed their snack bars after school and crumbs found their way to the floor. We are all enjoying my cute, curly haired little great-niece Leah Joy this afternoon. It's the first time we've gotten to babysit her, and we love it.

We decided to make pizza for supper. Maybe one of us can go to our deep freeze at the neighbor's and get ice cream to go with it.

We've had a good week—no accidents or sicknesses. We never know what the Lord has in store for us.

Saturday and *Sunday*. On Saturdays we normally do our weekly cleaning and often prepare food for the entire weekend. On Sundays we attend church. If it's a "Sunday in-between services" in our district, we might go to another district for church, invite company over for brunch or dinner, or spend a lazy day at home with the family.

People have commented to me about the amount of work we do in a day. I don't work more than any other farm wife and mother. It just happens that you see my schedule in black and white. I can't think of any other occupation I would rather be in. The Lord has been so good - to me. Let us bloom where we are planted!

◇◇◇◇◇

At the moment the house is quiet except for an occasional whispered "Mom" and a question from Jolisa, who is working in a preschool workbook. She's in front of the coal stove, which is everybody's favorite spot in the house. Jesse and Colleen are taking naps, and Wayne is outside feeding the cows. He will be in shortly to eat a warmed-up lunch. This forenoon he had gone to his brother Marion's to get a load of hay plus make a stop at a local feed store to get some calf feed, softener salt, and some potting soil for me.

Wayne's days as a full-time farmer are coming to an end. Our dashed hopes and dreams are about as cloudy as a dreary winter day. Yet on the other hand, we are very, very thankful after a prolonged time of job searching, praying, praying, and praying some more for God's leading and trusting to be led, Wayne has found a factory job. We will continue to milk cows and farm our land. We will all have to step up a notch and shoulder more responsibilities. As I said, this is not what we dreamed, but we are all ready for a change. It is necessary, and we are thankful for the job opportunity.

This new schedule will mean getting out of bed at 3:30 in the morning, bringing many changes in our routine. We are ready to give it our best shot. Wayne will get the brunt of this, and the children and I want to do our best to support him.

Colleen, Jolisa, and Jesse are enjoying our winter at home together. Joey (as some call Jolisa) and Jesse are pure sunshine—full of fun, playing so nicely together, being total little buddies. They get lots of attention from all the rest of us. You'd think they were babies. At the ages of six and four, they are a lot of fun.

This winter, a church friend asked if I'd host a tea party for her. I was flattered that she would ask me, and I nervously told her I would try. So we did. Colleen and I had a blast browsing through cookbooks and dreaming of how we would set it all up. We went to town, and then we went to work. We worked hard on preparations the day before. I skipped chores on the morning of the tea and still got very weak-kneed when the ladies arrived. Our wheels were spinning, but Colleen and I pulled it off! And we immensely enjoyed it. I love making things look attractive, so this truly was my cup of tea. Colleen also shares my passion for cooking, so this was a wonderful mother/daughter experience. The first was a brunch tea with 13 ladies, and then the second one was a lunch tea. Both were good. The brunch main courses were breakfast dishes, such as egg quiches, snowflake waffles, and calzones. The lunch tea main dishes were soups and sandwiches, plus all kinds of other goodies.

The second tea was extra special to me as it was the 10 ladies from our church who are in the same age group my mom was. These ladies go visit shut-ins and the elderly once a month, and the one whose turn it was to plan it surprised all the rest by treating them to a tea. It turned out to be a very snowy day, and their hired taxi driver did not want to go on the road. Two ladies who knew what was planned took their horses and buggies and picked up all the ladies and brought them here. What fun they had because they didn't know what all they were going to do.

First they visited a shut-in stroke patient. Usually they enjoy a coffee break there with her before they continue on their route, but that day no food was offered, adding to the mystery. Then they were brought here, and what a precious time we shared. It caused quite a few tears for us all, as these ladies were such a big part of Mom's life. She too always enjoyed their "visiting" days. We spent a lot of time reminiscing. My cup runneth over with their precious fellowship.

◇◇◇◇◇

Next week Jolisa will attend school a couple days. Preschool! How I remember the tough time I had of letting go when Colleen started school. And now our fifth child is ready to start, and Colleen has already completed her eight school years. The next thing I know I'll wake up old with my children all grown. I'm convinced time flies! I remember as a young married mother that I'd look up to those experienced mothers at the age of 35 or older and totally respect and admire them. Thinking at that age they'd really know what life was all about and be very knowledgeable in all aspects of life. Now I am 36 years old, and mostly I feel young and not nearly as mature and knowledgeable as those 35 year olds were 15 years ago.

◇◇◇◇◇

Colleen has invited some girlfriends over for supper and a sleepover tonight. It's our first experience of the sort at this age. The rest of the children are giving her a hard time—that she is so special she gets to have chips and pop. It's caused a lot of ruckus, but it's been a lot of fun. She wants to serve chili soup, ham-and-cheese calzones, and ice cream for supper. She wants cheese-and-egg quiche and waffles for brunch tomorrow.

◇◇◇◇◇

This winter we have gotten together with the neighbors several times to sing praises to our Lord. Sitting around the table and singing our hearts out with people our lives are entwined with is totally awesome. We love it. Big deal if you mess up, sing off-key, or sing when you aren't supposed to. Everybody does it once in a while. We all laugh and go on.

Talking about uplifting—I had the opposite happen to me lately...a real downer. Going on my walk one very snowy day, I was suddenly looking at the sky because my feet went south very quickly and my head went north. I was flat on my back before I even realized I was falling. Quickly I was on my feet again, checking to see if anybody had seen me. It didn't appear so. I thought I was fine until the next day. I was very sore and had a bit of a headache.

◇◇◇◇◇

I cooked a big batch of cornmeal mush to fry for brunch tomorrow. I will also throw together a brunch casserole or something of the sort, make sausage gravy, tomato gravy, cook some syrup, and bake a batch of cheese blitzes to round out the meal. Our friends Ervin and Esther will bring a pan of fried cornmeal mush and head cheese. We will enjoy a feast and warm friendship together. We prefer homemade pancake syrup, especially if I serve it warm.

Pancake Syrup

I simmer equal parts—let's say 2 cups each of brown sugar, white sugar, and water. Add approximately 1 cup white corn syrup and simmer a while. Once I turn off the heat, I add a few drops of maple flavoring.

You can tell I was taught to cook in a very approximate way. My mom would add a little of this and a bit of that, creating many wonderful dishes and daughters who are very daring in cooking. Now that is the way I am teaching my daughters. I hope they will all love cooking as much as all my sisters do.

◇◇◇◇◇

I will probably have a hard time getting the children out of bed this Monday morning. We had a lazy, restful day at home yesterday, so the children had a hard time settling down last night at bedtime. After being in bed a while, Jesse came down the stairs saying he messed his pants. "Whatever for?" I asked. "We were laughing too much, Mom!" he replied.

My word, it's time to settle down and sleep. So I cleaned him up and sent him back to bed with strict orders to be quiet and sleep. Around a half hour later, I detected a flashlight and four feet coming down the stairs, trying to be very quiet. It's almost as if they weren't breathing lest we hear them. All at once there was a loud crash, and I cringed. Now what? All is quiet. And then I heard some snorts and a suppressed giggle. Quietly, with not much expression, Karah said, "Daddy, the flashlight fell into the toilet." *Yuck!* Thankfully Wayne rose to that occasion and took care of the situation. It was late by then. Praise the Lord—it was peaceful the rest of the night!

◇◇◇◇◇

Now this morning the cows are milked, the calves are fed, the horses have their munchies, and Wayne is off to work. Colleen and Brian head back to bed again. All is quiet except for the hum of the gas lamps.

◇◇◇◇◇

Today is laundry day again, baking again, and clean up the house again. Isn't that just about as boring as life can get? With feeding nine mouths, it seems we are always preparing food. Especially to fill the four lunch pails, eat breakfast, have a snack when Wayne comes home from work and snacks when the children come home from school, and eat for supper. It's a never ending, "Mom, what's to eat?"

If our hearts are right with the calling we as mothers have from the Lord, we can have great *joy* in these mundane, everyday tasks we have to do. I cannot think of a more pleasant feeling than sitting down to eat with my family around the kitchen table and everyone digging in and polishing off the food set before them and joining in all the important family discussions. Our conversations range from belly-busting funny to very serious. Then we wash dishes again. We sweep the floor again. One day, and then the next day. Again and again. That's exactly what the Lord wants us to do, and what a wonderful, blessed, simply satisfying calling we have.

◇◇◇◇◇

I wish I could remember more what my mom used to bake while I was still at home. I think we usually had cookies, and we'd dunk those into our water for dessert. She also liked to bake pie. I guess I inherited that from her. For breakfast we usually had "dunk eggs,"* buttered bread, and cereal. Sometimes she would make tomato gravy and fried potatoes, pancakes, or fried cornmeal mush. In the wintertime, she'd make breakfast and put it on top of the warming shelf of her wood cookstove. That always looked and smelled so warm and inviting to come in to after choring. For lunch it was always meat, potatoes, and vegetables. For supper we had soup. Hot soup in the winter, and cold soup in the summer. On Saturday nights we had toasted cheese sandwiches and chocolate milk.

Mother's Day. I wish I would've made that day more special for Mom while I had the chance. I know she knew we loved her, but we all like to be told again and again.

Some of the earliest memories I have of Mom is taking naps with her at noon. She'd read a Raggedy Ann book to me and then we'd both fall asleep. It got to the point where she would fall asleep and I would slip away. I also remember at a young age sitting with her in church and putting my head on her lap to take a nap sometime during the three-hour services.

Secretly I've been wishing for new living room and bedroom flooring. Ours is worn down to bare wood in some places. It has so many nicks and scratches that it always looks very dirty. I keep a rug in the middle of the living room to cover most of it up plus help with warmth in the winter. Still I keep dreaming. I don't want to succumb to begging or nagging because I know it's not possible to change it now anyway. Why make life miserable?

I think of the floor Mom used to have here in the kitchen before they remodeled. One half was dark-red linoleum with a brick design, and the other half was a light-green color. Imagine. It was ugly. A real breech in modern interior design. Plus, the last several years it had a spot by the table measuring about two feet by two feet that was worn to the wood. She kept a rug thrown over it, which was very inconvenient at that particular spot. I don't recall hearing her complaining once. Mom and Dad did remodel then, and she had a nice floor. Maybe if

I am quietly patient like Mom, we can someday make improvements too. At least I have a warm cozy house to live in. The people down in Haiti...

Do we sometimes confuse what we want and what we really need? Are we the cause of peer pressure?

⬦⬦⬦⬦⬦

This week I want to work on cutting and sewing six pairs of denim pants and an unlined denim coat for Wayne—a job that has been necessary for a long time already. Colleen needs to finish up a quilt she has been piecing, plus I surprised her with fabric for a new dress so she can sew that this week.

Wednesday I have plans to spend the day with two friends, Linda and Ruth. We rarely see each other, so I'm really looking forward to spending the day with them.

Thursday evening Wayne wants to take Brian and Jesse to the horse sale. I'm hoping it works out because they rarely get to go to places like that.

⬦⬦⬦⬦⬦

Sometimes motherhood is overwhelming to me. It seems like I can't stretch in all the directions I should. Keeping my family fed and clothed, plus the most important...meeting all their emotional and spiritual needs can be hard. I rely wholly on the Lord for his guidance. I am nothing without him. I think of what Jesus said to Mary when Martha accused her of not doing enough: "She hath done what she could" (Mark 14:8). Oh, to have him say that about me!

Summer

There, now that's done. Wayne's work pants were almost falling to his knees, so I tightened them for him. Wayne can lose weight without even giving it a thought. In fact, I know some women who can do that too. I've been one of those lucky ones who come from a long lineage of weight-challenged women. I seem to be between a rock and a hard place.

I can chose to relax and simply eat whatever I want to and enjoy it to the max, which would be wonderful since I love to cook and bake delicious dishes. But then I'd have to deal with not feeling good physically and mentally. There are so many delicious-looking processed foods available on the market that are so tempting to weak people like me. I find it helps to shop locally where a little less variation is available. That's my rock.

Now the hard place is always having to make a great, conscious, thoughtful effort to what I eat in a day. To have been born in a long line of naturally thin ladies seems to me would eliminate a lot of stress. Actually, the big deal to me is to be healthy and physically fit. I come from a long line of people with heart and diabetes problems, and I'd like to do my part in avoiding these diseases.

I have no problem with getting enough exercise since I do chores for four hours a day. With our changed routine, I inherited more chores. It requires carrying and dumping five-gallon buckets of water. I immensely enjoy it. It gets my heart pumping and gives me energy.

Recently I was telling my children how I used to climb up into the silo to pitch down the silage, load the silage onto a wheelbarrow, and then push the full load about 75 feet out to the feeder. About 20 of those feet were on a two-by-eight-inch board that was suspended from the feed alley to the feed bunk (the area from silo to the place we fed the cows). Load after load after load I hauled. We had no skid loader then. I do think it made me wide awake and ready for school in the morning. We had to get up early to chore, but I'm guessing we handled it okay because we never had plans for evenings during the week. We did the chores, ate supper, maybe played a few card games with my mom and grandma, and went to bed early.

Wayne's been working in the fields after getting home from his job. Brian can do the TMR mixing, feeding, and other outside chores, plus whatever else we deem necessary to have done. I tackle the milking. Colleen keeps the house going with all that needs doing. The little girls help too wherever they're directed. One day leads into the next, and time keeps marching steadily on.

The last time we went to town, I treated the little ones to some candy. I also bought a fresh pineapple. That evening while cutting up the pineapple I had a hard time getting any into the bowl because little hands kept snatching the pieces as fast as I cut them. Jesse told me, "Mom, these are better than that candy!"

I agreed. I'm thankful they like fresh fruits and vegetables. Just now Colleen, Jolisa, and Jesse went in search of fresh asparagus, hoping there is enough for lunch tomorrow.

That squeaky, trusty, red trike has reached retirement age. Jesse took to riding a bike like a fish takes to water. His only handicap in the learning process has been starting off. We have a circle driveway the little ones can fly around on their bikes. It's fun to hear their imaginary stories of where they are going, often stopping in to see if we have this or that they can borrow, depending on the story. To have their sweet, sweet innocence...Sometimes their depth of thought scares me. They notice minute details and imitate them, good or bad. They definitely keep me humble.

One of my greatest concerns as a child was wanting a bike. An honest-to-goodness, two-wheeled bike. I had a trike but had outgrown that by two years. I remember kneeling to pray with my little brother Jay out under the two big maple trees. God was faithful—I did get one!

◇◇◇◇◇

I thought we had stress with dairy farming and trying to make an honest-to-goodness living. Add to that the stress of Wayne working at the RV factory. Add to that just life in general. Sometimes I feel like throwing up my hands, screaming at the top of my lungs, and running as fast as I can. Run where? I don't know, but run nonetheless. I know those are not healthy thoughts, but admit it—we've all had them.

I need to back up, sit up, and remember what all I have to be thankful for. Between my pinched-up, stressed-up, narrow eyes it too often looks like too little to me, and for those thoughts I am truly embarrassed. I *am* thankful for what we have: a family filled with love. And we are all healthy as far as I know. When we sit down at the supper table, we are all at home together. There is no way I can list all I am thankful for.

We need to pray to keep our healthy minds and our faith in God. We need to remember to relax and enjoy the blessings the Lord has so graciously given us.

◇◇◇◇◇

The smartest advice on raising children is to enjoy them while they are still on your side. I enjoyed that quote when I read it. It also makes a sigh escape my lips. They do not have to be very old before they form their own opinions, ideas, and characters. We've had some pretty bumpy days since summer vacation has started.

"Mom, we just washed dishes!" "It's Karah's turn, or it's Emily's turn, or it's Jolisa's turn." It's time to get a chart made so we can stay more organized and save us the fuss of all these petty arguments.

When we went to Wayne's home place the other evening, he teasingly encouraged me to get a handful of lilac twigs off the lilac bush. He remembers what those feel like on his hiney, and he thought maybe the girls should know too. I was going to take his advice seriously and then forgot. So I guess for now the rubber spatula will have to do.

This is the first full week that the scholars are at home. This morning Karah helped Colleen with a huge laundry. Friday night was Wayne's side of the family night, Saturday was the end-of-the-year picnic at the school, and Sunday night we went to see our brand-new niece, Deanna Kay. That meant a lot of laundry to do.

Early this morning Brian went to the field to *cultimulch.** He enjoys working in the fields, which is evident because he was soon in the field after lunch. Watching him hitch up those big Belgian draft horses— and evidently knowing what he was doing—had my heart by the strings. He'll be 14 in August and has much better insights on farming than I do...except for the milking part. He can milk, but he doesn't enjoy it.

◇◇◇◇◇

We've had a lot of rain lately, which on our farm produces mud. Major mud. Karah decided it's easier to go get the cows in from the pasture in bare feet than with boots. She lost her boots to the mud one time. It's easier washing her feet.

◇◇◇◇◇

We had a hard frost this morning. Wayne was quite concerned about the hay. It's looking good at knee-high and higher. We are hoping for a good harvest. He plans on making *haylage** with the first cutting.

I've had to rinse frost off the strawberry patch a couple mornings. I want to save all the strawberries I can. We are looking forward to strawberries and ice cream, strawberry shortcake...well, just about anything is good with fresh strawberries—even salads.

◇◇◇◇◇

I'm sitting here with a blue bandana wrapped around my neck and smelling like a Vick's VapoRub jar. Last week Wayne started out with a bad head cold. He didn't have one all winter. Having a cold in this warm weather is miserable. Now I've started with a bad sore throat, earaches, and sniffles. With my sister Freda coming from Oklahoma this week, it produces a lot of plans, so I'm hoping this bug is short-lived. The girls are actually getting to the end of the dirty dishes. We need to continue working on the virtue of promptness. It's amazing all the things they can do at the same time. The stories they come up with are worth recording, as are the songs they sing. The squabbles we can forget.

Karah is now baking a couple pans of cookies. This morning I stirred a big batch of chocolate chip cookies together to bake some now and then later this week. I usually bake them all at once, but with Freda coming I decided to bake them fresh as needed. We're excited to have her in our midst.

◇◇◇◇◇

The other evening after supper and playing outside for a good while, Jesse was hungry and simply had to have something to eat. We prepared a small bowl of yogurt and granola for him. He sat on the couch and devoured it, savoring it to the last lick. Then out loud he said to himself, "Was that good, boy?" He paused and then he said, "Yes, it was!" We all got a good laugh out of that.

We've been teaching Jesse to talk English, which is always interesting to me. I remember before I was old enough to go to school I told one of my dad's friends, "It is dropping!" It had started to rain. The less I talk English, the more Dutchy I get.

We have the absolute ugliest county dirt roads we've ever had. They are supposedly graveled, but this spring they dumped tons of stones on them. It's almost impossible to ride a bike on them, and that's a major form of transportation for us. With our house practically on the road, we eat a lot of dust.

We appreciate when it rains so the dust is settled and the vehicles pack the stones so it's easier to bike on and easier for the horse to pull the buggy. Our appreciation doesn't last really long because it seems as soon as it rains the workers come by with a big grader and tear the stones all up again. Hopefully one of these days they'll put some dust control on the roads again. That always helps for most of the summer. I appreciate living in the country, and for the most part of the day our road is fairly quiet. The mornings and afternoons are busy with factory traffic and school buses.

Some days Wayne comes home from work late, so we trudge on, putting in long hours. I feel very fortunate to be able to work, and I do not want to complain. Spring and summer are my favorite seasons, even if we work long, hard days. I have hopes of leisure nights sitting around the campfire in our yard and enjoying s'mores and popcorn. The children spend a lot of time on the trampoline in the evenings— so much so that we sometimes have to use the timer so everyone gets an equal opportunity. Even this mama likes a turn. That's good because I need to burn those calories from all those strawberries and ice cream and s'mores.

I've started doing my walking in the morning since it gets daylight earlier. I love listening to the birds' cheery good-morning songs, plus it is a time completely to myself. Colleen and Brian both go back to bed after the chores are done, but all too soon it is time to get everyone up and at it.

◇◇◇◇◇

I am anxiously awaiting canning season as I'm out of ketchup, and I noticed the tomato juice is getting low. I thought I had done a lot last year, but I guess it takes a lot too. The apple pie filling is also getting low, so I'd better start using more of the other fillings. Apple seems to be a favorite. We use the apple filling for apple crisp too. We dump a quart of the filling in a baking dish, top it with our homemade granola, and bake it until it is heated through. You can't get it any simpler or yummier than that!

◇◇◇◇◇

The last several days we have been crossing a lot of odd jobs off our list of have-to-be-done. That's a good feeling. We're not caught up, but we sure enjoy making a dent in the list. This summer I've been making lists every day or two, and that seems to be working well. The girls think all they have to do is wash the dishes and sweep the floor. I keep telling them that is the way to learn to work and to like it—by knowing the satisfaction of a job well done. We adults have to do the same things over and over and over. Suppose we would decide one day we just don't want to anymore? That advice lasts for one complaint. How quickly the children forget. They helped really well with cleaning strawberries. Bringing in the laundry from the lines and folding and putting it away is about the worst punishment to them. But it's a job that has to be done, and they can easily do it.

◇◇◇◇◇

I'm having a bad case of fingernail-biting nervousness right now with a field of raked hay waiting to be baled. Wayne is still not at home. Our neighbor Junior will be here in a couple minutes, as will several more neighbor boys to help. I don't like to make them wait. Brian does really well with harnessing and hitching up the horses, getting the hay raked, and all that, but sometimes the know-how and management skills of mine are pretty well zilch. When we see Wayne coming home, Brian and I breathe huge sighs of relief. It feels so good when we are all at home and working together.

◇◇◇◇◇

The other morning I slept a little too long, so I was in the parlor by myself a little while longer than normal. It was dark and rainy, which made me tired and moody. I was thinking of all the rain, all the mud, and planting crops late because of it. Must be I needed a wakeup call from my self-pitying thoughts because all of a sudden a cat let out a horrible scream! It grabbed my attention.

I kept on hosing out the milk parlor, and my mind started to wander again. Then two male cats got into a vicious fight. They really got my attention off me! I proceeded to give them a good morning shower with the startling cold water. They took their fighting elsewhere, and I continued on with the chores. As Colleen would say, that's about as exciting as our life gets.

◇◇◇◇◇

We have this little bull we've been feeding to fatten up to butcher next year. His name is Hamburger Steak. Well, he discovered he's quite the macho man once he got to the cows. The excitement level got plenty high the other night when Brian and I were milking. Hamburger Steak thought he belonged in the parlor with us. He had plenty of bawling and aggressiveness to get where he wanted. It made my heart pound and my knees weak. My legs turned to rubber. A bull is nothing to mess with. Needless to say, as soon as Wayne came home Hamburger Steak got moved back to where he belonged. That's plenty of excitement for me!

I have a peace rose that hasn't bloomed for several years, but it has such beautiful foliage so I keep the plant. It turns out the foliage is wild, and it has bloomed profusely this summer—only the blooms aren't the peace rose. They are a cheery, bright red. Big deal. I'm not professional either. We might as well bloom where we are planted. The other roses are busy bringing sunshine to our lives. We have four rosebushes where we can see them from the kitchen window. The hummingbirds also frequent the feeder right outside that window. It makes washing the dishes a bit more interesting.

◇◇◇◇◇

We didn't get our fill of asparagus this spring, much to the chagrin of the children. They brought in enough for some soup the other evening. It was barely enough for that, but we made do. Growing an asparagus patch takes patience, but it will multiply. We just have to be patient. The strawberries were delicious while they lasted. Now we are looking forward to fresh blueberry pie. We're hoping to enjoy the fresh blueberry pie with our friends the Hogues from Oklahoma. We're looking forward to their annual visit.

◇◇◇◇◇

On my daily walk this morning I heard the birds singing their praises. I saw a new species! It looked like a scarlet tanager, but I don't know if those are in this area or not. It was a beautiful, bright red-orange. I also heard the woodpeckers busily at work. Taking a morning walk has many benefits. It helps keep my mind clear and often fills my heart with song.

◇◇◇◇◇

This spring Wayne and I went on several dates again. What fun and oh so romantic. After I was done with the evening milking, I'd walk back to the field and join him on the plow for several rounds to catch up on the daily news. No roses. No fancy, expensive dinner. But love and partnership to the fullest! Yep, Wayne is mighty popular when he comes home from work. I walk up to the house again, and there by the walkway to the house are the roses, and Colleen has prepared us supper, I am blessed indeed.

We love these long summer evenings, but they do have a big disadvantage. We have a hard time knowing when to stop working and go to bed. So soon it is time to get up again. We do take time for making s'mores though, and lounging around the campfire, and gazing at the stars, and filling a jar with fireflies.

Did you ever make s'mores with Ritz Crackers instead of graham crackers? We love it! Ritz Crackers, Hershey's Milk Chocolate bars, and roasted marshmallows. What a way to end the day!

Fall

Some days I really wonder why we even want to dairy farm. I really struggle to keep my focus. Some days things happen...

Wayne's at work, it looks like a fifty–fifty chance of rain, and there's hay on the ground ready to rake and bale. Should we rake it or should we not? Should we rake it or should we not? We don't want it raked if it'll rain on it before we get it baled. Should we rake it or should we not? Lord, I really need your guidance. Help me make the wisest decision. We didn't do too badly.

◇◇◇◇◇

Friday morning, 4:45, almost time for Wayne to head to the house. We had the milkers on the second batch of cows when Wayne suddenly bolted from the parlor and ran for the motor room. The diesel was making some awfully loud noises. Wayne checked things out and started the diesel again with me standing behind him praying for deliverance. Wayne promptly shut the motor off.

By that time it was dangerously close to the time Wayne had to get ready to go to his day job. I called our neighbor lady, asking if she could take me to go get the repairman. The repairman came back with us, sacrificing his morning. I totally dreaded his verdict. "Ruined," that's what I heard. Totally overhaul or buy brand-new. One would cost as much as the other. Lord, what are you trying to tell us? I admit I had some unhealthy thoughts going through my mind.

Most of the cows weren't milked. I think they were totally confused because cows are creatures of habit. About 8:00 I biked to our faithful friends to see if we could put our herd over to theirs until we got our mess straightened out. They had also milked our herd for six weeks some years back when our old barn was struck by lightning and burned to the ground. They, of course, said we could.

By that time we figured it could go a week until we have power again. Power, oh my! How soon will we be without water pressure? Our diesel also powers the air compressor that supplies the air for our water supply.

Our friend's eldest son biked to the phone shack to call his uncle who has a truck and trailer to see if he could come haul our cows to their farm. He said he could be there in an hour. I biked home again and gulped down a banana and some yogurt and granola so I would have some energy again.

I told Karah and Emily to just fill the washing machine halfway to conserve water. And to please use the outhouse instead of the toilet. We need to save all the water we can. Later Wayne thought I'd overreacted a bit, but, hey, I'm just this meek little lady trying to do the job of a man. Something I most certainly cannot do.

Colleen was cleaning house. Both ours and Dad's had to be cleaned. Karah and Emily were doing the laundry alone for the first time because they simply had to. We discovered they easily could! They just had a small amount, and they enjoyed doing it. Brian was back in the field getting it ready for Wayne to plant corn that evening. He had to stay at it.

The little girls were soon done with the laundry and came out to help me get the cows in from the fields again. Joe came with his truck and backed up to the sliding door. The girls and I tried to get the cows onto the truck. Come on laugh—because it was a joke! Me trying to load cows onto a stock trailer! I hate doing something like that because I am not good at it at all. Karah was immediately covered with manure from the top of her head to her feet. Poor thing. About the only clean area on her were the whites of her eyes, and those looked *very* white. She looked at me totally shocked because I just had to laugh. It was either laugh or cry, so laugh I did.

The cows didn't want to cooperate. I wanted to despair, but I kept praying for wisdom. *Aha!* I know what I will do. We put the cows into the holding pen and made an alleyway from the parlor to the trailer. It actually worked! The cows were eager to be milked, so we tricked them. It took three jags to get our little herd moved. After the last ones were loaded, I joked that maybe the sale barn would be hiring now that I could actually load cows. Now, had it been auction day...well, just a thought I had better not dwell on.

We rushed about getting our other work done. At 3:30 I went to the neighbors' place to help them milk their cows and ours. Esther, their daughter Erma, and I had a total rodeo—free of charge, at that. Ervin's dad finally came and helped a bit, and we actually got the 80-plus cows milked before Wayne or Esther's husband got there to help. It was a long two hours, and we weren't totally positive that we'd gotten them all milked because several might have cleared the fence. We really didn't care; we had all we could handle.

We did get the diesel motor on the next Monday. We brought the cows home on Monday night after chores. I had finally calmed down a little. I didn't even enjoy my so-called vacation from choring each day. Wayne went over to help Ervin with the milking over the weekend. I did remind myself that none of us was hurt or sick, and this too shall pass. Life just keeps me wondering...

◇◇◇◇◇

That Saturday we had some visitors from Ohio. That's why our house and Dad's had to be cleaned. These visitors were Andy Weaver and his daughter Naomi, her husband, Robert, and son Adam. It has been wonderful getting to know the Andy Weaver family. Andy lost his wife the same year we lost Mom. Our families have a lot of similarities. Our parents are the same ages; we siblings are the same ages as theirs; and all the way down to minute details like both our fathers eating the same kind of cereal for breakfast. I have finally, after talking on the phone the last two years, met Andy's daughter Rhoda and her family. She is my age, lives on the home dairy farm with her dad in a small house just like us. They have been a wonderful blessing to my family.

Canning season is here again. Colleen and I cleaned out the basement and took inventory of all we need to can yet. Now, if only we could keep that dungeon clean all the time.

The bean crop was good, so we were done canning those in a hurry because we could do a lot at a time. We also did a lot of black raspberry pie filling and jelly. We don't need to do any blueberry filling, but we had to get some blueberries for fresh eating and fresh pie.

We've been eating a lot of cucumbers, and kohlrabi, and yellow summer squash (our favorite!). We love the squash fried and then put on buttered bread with a slice of Muenster cheese. Tastes like summer!

While sitting at the table eating lunch, the little girls hang their spoons on their noses acting like clowns. Yes, they literally hang their spoons on their noses, and the spoons stay there. They do get their food eaten after we've laughed a while.

School is in full swing again. Sure seems quiet with just Colleen, Jesse, and me at home during the day. We just kind of picnic for lunch, having the main meal at supper time again. Jolisa is in first grade this year, Emily in second, Karah in fourth, and Brian in the eighth. My mom would love the stages our children are in right now.

We're cleaning house again. Church comes around every seven months. It was time to do some deep cleaning again anyway. I am so glad for the privilege of hosting services, for more reasons than cleaning, but I don't know how else we would get the cleaning done. I don't always wash all the walls and such because it's our turn so often. With doing some each time, it doesn't get so bad either. While cleaning the upstairs, the children wanted to rearrange their furniture, so we took time to do that. I've always liked to rearrange, but our house isn't big enough and doesn't leave me with a whole lot of options.

Here on the main floor I just keep it the same old way, but I do have my own way of fighting boredom. I rearrange the decorations I have, like the things I have on the countertops and the houseplants. I don't have much else. Just enough to have it feel cozy but keep it simple and easy to clean.

◇◇◇◇◇

Our potato crop was a total failure this year. The red ones did do okay, but I finally told Brian to till the keeper potatoes under. It was embarrassing. We fought the bugs. They were so bad the plants didn't even get to the blooming stage. Usually if we wait to plant potatoes until mid to late June we can be pretty much bug free. Not this year. We picked bugs, we dusted bugs, we sprayed bugs, and we still had bugs. The dead bugs dropped to the ground, disappeared into holes in the ground (we could see the holes), and I think hatched thousands more to keep up their army. We admit that this year we lost. We'll try again next year. I guess it's not so bad. With gardening now for 17 years, this is the first it went like this.

We did have excellent muskmelons and watermelons. We ate them as fast as we could and wished they'd lasted longer. As we grow older it seems the growing season keeps getting shorter. When I was a child I thought I had to hoe the garden forever until we could finally empty it and enjoy other projects. Now we hoe it several times and, poof!, the season is over. I do know using a tiller helps make less hoeing. We used a horse-drawn cultivator back then, and we couldn't get as close to the plants as we can with a tiller. I also know the time goes faster as I get older.

Jesse was lucky enough to go with Wayne and me on a mini vacation to Holmes County, Ohio, this past summer. The others had to stay home. He keeps talking about those hills that Holmes County is so famous for. Every time we go up a gentle rise (that's all Indiana has compared to Ohio), he comments that this hill isn't like Ohio's, right? One day he was saying we should all go to see Sister Freda in Oklahoma. He paused just slightly and then replied, "But I would stay at home."

"Why would you stay at home?" I wondered.

"Well, I do not want to go to hills like that again!"

I explained that Oklahoma doesn't have hills like Ohio does.

One day Brian was bringing up the horses with Jesse tagging along as usual. Finally Jesse said he was tired and could hardly go anymore—and there was still half an inch to go.

Mid July, Wayne and I made a very difficult decision. We sold the cows. We decided to go with feeding heifers in the dairy barn and small calves in the shed part of the other barn. We will continue to farm, but now our chores have changed. The change is hard to put into words. It seemed doors kept closing for us, and we had to let them close for others to open.

We have set goals we hope to meet in the long run. Making improvements in the dairy barn and then reinvesting in a Jersey dairy herd. We realize this won't be in the near future.

The little girls came in saying they were watching the barn swallows swoop down close to their heads. In the evening the swallows are really busy catching bugs in the air. They put on quite a show. The hummingbirds also got very bold this year. They got used to us coming and going close to their feeder. All too soon they will be leaving us again. Oh, how I enjoy the summer! To me fall is so sad. Yes, beautiful in its own way, but I love summer so much it's always sad to see it end.

Tomorrow I am going on a little outing. I really should stay at home and work, but I'll get up really early and work as fast as I can so I can then go and relax. A longtime family friend from Kalamazoo, Michigan, will pick up my sisters and me, and we'll go to Das Dutchman Essenhaus for lunch and a time of catching up with everybody. A special time for all of us. This lady and her husband were the second customers for my Grandmother Raber's quilt business. A lot of water has gone under the bridge since that time. Thousands of quilts have been made, sold, and enjoyed. The business has been a huge blessing in our extended family for years. My grandmother was widowed at a young age, and this was her livelihood.

◇◇◇◇◇

This forenoon I went to town for groceries. That's a challenge for me. I'm more stressed out and tired after getting groceries than if I'd stay home and worked really hard all day. I try to be a very careful shopper, and by the time I'm done my brain feels like mush.

Colleen cleaned the bedroom walls, ceiling, furniture, and woodwork while I was gone. She also scrubbed the living room furniture. As ugly as it is, the only way we can tell it's been cleaned is because we know it. But, hey, at least we have a house to live in. That's a lot more than countless people can say. Keeps me humble.

Hamburger Steak keeps growing bigger. I keep envisioning all the packages of hamburger that will fill our freezer. He's pretty good at intimidating me; I'm downright scared of him. I'll be glad when he's meat.

One night after spending a very pleasant evening at Wayne's brother Gaylord's house, we came home and Sam the dog wasn't around. That was unusual as he's an extremely faithful welcoming committee. Usually he greets us as we turn into our driveway and proceeds to do a boogeyman search by all the buildings, ending up meeting us in front of the buggy shed as we stop, overjoyed to have us home again. But this time Sam did not come to meet us. The panic of losing him rose in our throats. I know he is just a dog, but he is our Sam. He is very much a part of our family.

The calling and searching were on. We were met with silence. Is it okay to pray to God to save our Sam? I sure did! Wayne checked in the milk house, and one happy Sam greeted him—glad to be set free again. I'd been the one who forgot to let him out of the milk house after I was done with the chores. We all slept peacefully.

"This is the day which the LORD hath made; we will rejoice and be glad in it" (Psalm 118:24). This verse often melodies through my mind in the morning.

I'm having a hard time getting all the sand out of my eyes this morning. Hopefully sipping some coffee will help a bit. For some reason I was extra tired last night, and I got out of bed this morning feeling like I had been run through a mill. Maybe this is why...

Two days ago my friend Virginia and I went to Schoolcraft, Michigan, to harvest grapes. I'd heard we could get them for a very reasonable price, and usually, people told me, a person can pick a bushel in just a matter of minutes. But this year frost got 75 percent of the crops, so it took quite a bit longer to pick three bushels. We took our leisurely time cutting the grapes and sorting out the bad ones. We paid by the pound and didn't want to pay for bad ones. It was after lunch when we were done. We stopped at McDonald's to grab a bite to eat on the way home. We had seen a Goodwill store on the way up in the morning, so we decided we almost *had* to stop if we were that close.

All told, we didn't get home until 3:30 in the afternoon. After settling all of Wayne and the children's curiosities about my day, and after I had listened to the events of their day, I dashed about and steamed two batches of grapes in the steamer/juicer. By then it was time to head to the neighborhood ice-cream social.

The next morning, before filling Wayne's lunch bucket, I got another steamer going with grapes. I knew it would take all day, so I thought I had best get started.

While preparing the children's breakfast, I put together a simple brunch casserole for a neighbor lady. Colleen and Karah delivered that, and then went on to another neighbor's place to borrow another juicer/ steamer. (I'd be lost without my neighbors.)

After breakfast Colleen started with tomatoes. She canned around 30 quarts of tomato juice. I washed and steamed grapes all forenoon. And washed dishes...and more dishes. You should have seen our kitchen. Between my grapes, Colleen's tomatoes, and Jesse's toys, we had it looking quite lived in! As the day progressed, we had stacks of empty 5-gallon buckets and 10-gallon tubs outside the kitchen door waiting to be washed. By noon we had it where we thought we could kick up our feet a couple minutes until the next batch of grapes were steamed and the tomato juice was done steaming in the *Conservo.** Colleen went upstairs to her room, Jesse was on the couch looking at books, and I had just lifted my weary legs and stretched out on our bed (it felt so good!), when I heard a bawl and a low rumble of...*what* did I hear?

I sprang out of bed, looked out the window, and for a second I froze. *Horrors!* One of my worst nightmares was horrendously coming true. There, dancing in my sister Ida's yard and standing between our two houses, was a heifer and our large, menacing bull. "I am so afraid of him. Terribly afraid of him. He's big, he's black, and he is on the loose! Oh, Lord, help me!" I cried out. I screamed for Colleen and told Jesse he must absolutely not leave the house!

What else could I do but go outside? I searched for weapons, finding a flimsy rod of some kind and a crooked broom.

I went outside and ran to open the gate to a pasture; hopefully, I could get him in there. I wasn't concerned about the heifer. She looked quite harmless.

By that time, 42 heifers were lined up along the fence east of Ida's house to watch the show. Hamburger Steak was showing his stuff, doing his best to impress them.

Then the UPS truck came. Never was I so glad to see Mark, the UPS man! I told him we desperately need help. He drove east so he could hopefully keep the bull and heifer from running that way.

By now the bull was acting mad, thrashing and roving around like only a mad bull can. He butted heads with the heifer and then thrashed around again. He pawed up cornstalks that were scattered in the garden.

We were useless. Colleen went to the closest neighbors to see if they were home. Even though I had been praying constantly, by that time I was praying out loud desperately.

There is a crossroad about one-eighth mile east of here, and about that time a truck was headed south. I made enough motions that, praise the Lord, the guy saw me and hesitated. I motioned some more. He backed up and came to help. I told him what was up, where the two varmints belonged, and asked if he could use the truck to try to get them in.

Colleen and neighbor Leonard and his son were back by this time. The UPS man left to get more help. With the trucker's patient maneuvering of his truck and a good-sized landscaping stone landing between the eyes of Hamburger Steak as a distraction, they got him and the heifer to where they belonged. Praise God!

I was one shaky lady and so thankful that we were all unharmed. Hopefully Hamburger Steak will go to the sale barn today, and we'll use the profits to buy a nice, calm butcher steer to fill our freezer.

While we were still outside, we happened to think of our steamers going full blast in the house. Colleen ran and shut off the burners.

Now, when we came back inside, I checked the clock. We'd been outside barely an hour. It seemed quite a bit longer!

In the afternoon we made a triple-batch of pizza sauce. I was close to becoming claustrophobic in my messy kitchen. The counters were loaded with dirty dishes, ingredients, can lids, and whatever else that goes with canning. We had a six-foot table set up in the area of my cupboards and stove, so that made it a bit cramped, but we needed it to hold the canning jars.

All said and done, we processed 97 quarts by that evening. I was so thankful for the food and that the jobs were completed. Next on the canning list is applesauce and apple pie filling. We'll be glad when those messes are cleaned up and the cans all carried to the basement. After carrying the last cans of the season to the basement, I like to step back and look at the can shelves, my heart overflowing with gratitude.

By the time the dishes were all in their appropriate places again, the floors swept and mopped, supper eaten, and dishes washed again, it was time to shower and head for bed. I was afraid I'd have nightmares with Hamburger Steak chasing me, but I didn't. I slept solid.

◇◇◇◇◇

When we stopped at Goodwill the other day, I was lucky to find Brian some school shirts. All the shirts he had for school were blue, and these were yellow and cream. We were both happy about that. Today I want to pick off the pockets to make them appropriate to wear in our community. Colleen will launder the shirts and then they will be ready to wear.

◇◇◇◇◇

I mentioned earlier about making a casserole for a neighbor lady. Our church has a granite roaster that travels, filled, from house to house, being a continuous blessing. Whoever had church services last fills it for the lady who is preparing to host next. This gift is like sunshine on a busy day. We also have a cookie jar traveling along through the community. With a family to feed, it really helps out.

◇◇◇◇◇

Today I would like to change pace and do something totally different. Sew! I haven't sewn anything in the last two months. I guess I still know how. The children's requests for clothes have been getting loader and louder. I don't blame them. I know they each need several sets of new clothes. They keep on growing.

Winter

"Joy to the world the Lord is come. Let earth receive her king...Silent night, holy night, all is come, all is bright...Away in a manger no crib for a bed, the little Lord Jesus lay down his sweet head..." It's Christmastime, and I love the sounds of the season. Singing these old hymns is soothing to my mind and body. They bring peace to my soul. The news of Jesus' birth is as precious now as it was more than 2000 years ago. Jesus is alive!

Our Christmas church services are much the same as any other Sunday. Of course, the Christmas story from Scripture is used. Instead of our usual lunch of peanut-butter spread, jam, pickles, red beets, ham, cheese, and cookies, we have a "carry in lunch" we all enjoy. The people who host that day provide ham and pots of chicken noodles. Scalloped potatoes, vegetables, salads, Christmas Ribbon salad, and pies are brought in by everyone else. Sometimes we sing Christmas hymns in the afternoon; other times we visit with everyone before heading home filled to the brim spiritually and physically.

Hosting Wayne's family Christmas is a highly anticipated event. With close to 100 people, including his mom and dad, siblings, grandchildren, and greats, it takes a bunch of tables and chairs to accommodate everyone. Everyone comes with arms overloaded with food and games.

We fry pans of cornmeal mush, make breakfast quiches or casseroles, and cook biscuits, sausage gravy, tomato gravy, hash browns, ham and sausage, fruits, and pastries. We provide the meat and drinks, and the rest is provided by family members. It takes a lot of coffee and hot chocolate too.

After eating brunch around 8:30, we usually all sit down to sing Christmas carols. Sometimes we play a type of Bingo with Christmas gifts, but oftentimes we don't give gifts because each family shares gifts in their own home. The rest of the day is spent in fellowship and playing games.

In the afternoon, tables are laden with all sorts of homemade candies, fruits, vegetables, dips and snacks. Anything imaginable is there. We go home knowing we won't be needing supper—only exercise and water.

A day well spent creating memories and staying bonded with the extended family.

◇◇◇◇◇

It seems the older I get, the more I dread the cold of winter. I am always cold, which even to me is laughable because of the good-natured ribbing I dished out to some of my cousins and my dad. I never imagined I would someday be in their shoes. The first 15 years of marriage I often had a child or two on my lap. I usually had a fussy baby, a busy toddler or two to run after, plus plenty of extra padding on my body. Thus, oftentimes I was red-faced and warm. The last several years both scenarios have changed, and I often find myself scrambling for a jacket. The most unthinkable of all is wearing a long-sleeved nightgown and booties to bed. I must really be getting old.

With eight, thickly bundled people squashed into our antiquated surrey buggy, it brings on some chaos I like to avoid by just staying at home on cold winter nights. That can't always be done though, so we squeeze, grunt, and complain our way into the buggy and pray for a safe and peaceful trip to wherever we are headed.

There are things I do enjoy about winter. Piecing a quilt or two, doing some painting on greeting cards, sewing for the family, and eating chili for supper. Long, cozy evenings spent with the family. Feeling the warmth of the coal stove on my back as I relax with a good book in front of the stove.

A while back, in the wee hours of the morning, Colleen and I took the horse and buggy to our friends' house. There we joined Ruth and her daughter Julie in their buggy and headed toward Goshen. Our first stop was at Menards, where we loaded up on paint supplies for Colleen's bedroom. From there we drove to Walmart. After securing the horse to the hitching rail, we went in search of a city bus schedule. We'd made plans to travel to the Dunlap area to sate our daughters' shopping appetites. I wished to satisfy my curiosity about traveling this route via bus too.

As we waited by the first bus...with no driver in sight, Julie decided to deposit some of our jackets in the buggy before traveling on. She ran to the buggy and while there, the bus driver appeared and was going to leave immediately. The three of us on the bus begged the driver to wait, saying Julie is coming, running, please wait. We played our parts well; the driver stopped the bus. Talk about some country bumpkins trying to act like city folk.

After shopping at a used clothing store near the Dunlap Walmart, we ran to catch the bus again. No driver in sight again, but we dared not venture lest we miss out again. Then this bus was headed in the wrong direction so we had 30 minutes to browse in Walmart. I found boots for Emily and Jolisa at very decent prices. We headed out to the bus stop again, and this time the driver was an elderly, friendly fellow who answered some of our questions. We told him to drop us off at Kohl's. Okay, no problem, he says. We settled into our seats, expecting to travel several miles. Well, we traveled the same direction we had just run from, traveled around the building, and went directly into the Kohl's parking lot. We experienced a major fit of giggles!

We could easily have walked to Kohl's and saved us each a dollar. We were definitely fish out of water. The driver probably had the laugh of his day.

We had a good mother/daughter day, albeit exhausting. We did find our way home again, although much to Wayne's chagrin not until supper time. It was fun while it lasted, but I am glad it doesn't happen often. I was tired.

◇◇◇◇◇

I'd much rather work a hard day of labor at home, surrounded by familiar, simple things, and be at peace. In fact, Wayne and I just got done vaccinating 48 steers. I thoroughly enjoyed that job. For some reason I smelled a lot worse than when I was used to milking cows twice a day, but I loved it anyway. Brian and Emily helped too. Jesse and Jolisa played in the feed while we were vaccinating, and what a mess Jesse was! He had to change clothes in the washhouse before coming on into the house, but he did it willingly because his daddy told him he could go to a farm store open house with him.

It still seems so different to not be doing chores four hours a day. Brian does the chores in the morning: feeding the heifers, steers, horses, and Sam the dog. That arrangement works fine as long as we don't have frozen water pipes and the tractor and skid loader start.

In the afternoon, Wayne comes home from work around 1:30, eats a bit, and heads outside to do whatever has to be done. There is always plenty to do. One dark Friday morning, when Wayne wasn't working at the factory, he discovered our small heifers were missing. The evening before Sam had barked several times, but we figured it was just because of the vehicles passing by. Sam doesn't bark without reason. The heifers had probably been out then already. Wayne searched a while in the dark, but gave up until daylight. I guess it was their turn to go camping, as they had nested down in the ditch beside the road, east and south of us. We were thankful nobody hit them, as they could have caused a lot of injuries or worse.

◇◇◇◇◇

A 21-year-old lady caused quite a stir around here the other Saturday morning. Our girls noticed my dad walking up the road a bit, and he was working with a horse that appeared to be in distress. We finally figured out it was a dumped buggy. Her horse had spooked about something beside the road, upset the buggy, trapping her underneath. About that time, this young gal was at our house needing help. She could hardly talk, but said she thought her jaw was broken. I totally agreed with her, as her jaw was disfigured.

Our girls ran here and there getting her paper towels, and then the girls disappeared. I prayed for guidance. I felt like a jack rabbit jumping here and there trying to help her, cleaning her up a bit, hoping to keep her as comfortable as possible.

A lady soon came to take her to the hospital. This young lady ended up being transported from one hospital to the next in an ambulance. She needed surgery to fix her crushed jaw. She also lost four teeth and more were loose. She needed between 80 and 100 stitches in her mouth. Had I known the extent of her injuries, I probably would have fainted. I was impressed with her calmness.

I believe when these things happen, God has a plan. I was thankful to be here for her, but I had to wonder what the purpose was. It happened here for a reason. She came to our door for a reason. What was I to learn? I pray our hearts are always open. During devotions I came across Matthew 25:35-40:

> For I was an hungred, and ye gave me meat: I was thirsty, and ye gave me drink: I was a stranger, and ye took me in: Naked, and ye clothed me: I was sick, and ye visited me: I was in prison, and ye came unto me. Then shall the righteous answer him, saying, Lord, when saw we thee an hungred, and fed thee? or thirsty, and gave thee drink? When saw we thee a stranger, and took thee in? or naked, and clothed thee? Or when saw we thee sick, or in prison, and came unto thee?

And the King shall answer and say unto them, Verily I say unto you, Inasmuch as ye have done it unto one of the least of these my brethren, ye have done it unto me.

On Thanksgiving Day our family gained a family member when Dad and Alice Borkholder were united in marriage. As life goes on, we experience one change after the other. We trust in God to lead us, and we trod onward, one step at a time and make the best of every situation.

Throughout this last year, I kept telling myself it's not always the situations we are in that control our lives, but what we chose to make of the situations. My attitude is 99 percent of everything!

Where would I be without Jesus? Where would I spend eternity? Lost in a world full of sadness without Jesus, where would I be?

We as American people are so blessed to be able to go to town—the town of our choice—to do our grocery shopping. So why then does it make me so tired? Decisions, decisions. So many choices, and it flattens the checkbook in such a short time. Do we buy healthy or unhealthy, store brand or name brand, fresh or frozen?

I watch prices like a hawk and can smell a good deal from a mile away, but that doesn't always mean I buy it. I still ask myself, "Is this really necessary?" Sometimes I splurge, but most times, by the time I have the regular items like soup crackers, lunch meat, butter, flour, sugar, and such, the cart is piled high and the receipt is a foot-and-a-half long. Grocery shopping in the winter is even worse. My children are horrified by the way I look when I go to town: thick black socks, several jackets under my too-big coat, a thick head scarf, plus an outer bonnet over that. Fashion statement failure deluxe.

"Mom, are you really going to town like that?"

Riding seven miles in the buggy, tying up the horse at least four times, walking hither and yon, I get cold. Therefore I dress to stay warm, fashionable or not. The girls went to school anyway and forgot about me.

◇◇◇◇◇

Wayne says we need to vaccinate calves again today. I kind of enjoy that. Being outside in the barn, working together, getting fresh air. The exercise feels wonderful to me. Wayne would probably laugh at me. Exercise for me while vaccinating calves? All I do is hold a gate, hand him a syringe that I had filled, and then open the gate to release the calf. Two steps forward, two steps back, fill the syringe, two steps back, on and on. I've never danced, but maybe this is kind of like dancing in the barn with my husband.

Sam, our yellow Lab, enjoys helping out wherever he can. Sometimes, though, he's better off not being around when sorting cattle is involved, as he gets too excited. He's very much a part of our family, making us feel safe with his regular search route when we come home at night.

Recently Colleen didn't get home until late at night, and Sam was already in his bedroom, thus she was alone to put away the horse. Usually Sam goes with her, and she feels protected. I grew up with a dog like that. A small rat terrier named Tiny. If he would have growled when I was putting my horse in the barn at night, I would have panicked. When he didn't, I relaxed, knowing as sensitive as he was, he would alert me to any danger. Sam is the same way. A dog worth having—and we only paid $20 for him.

When nobody is outside to be with Sam, he's usually on the front-door steps either relaxing or looking in with big, soulful eyes longing to be in the house with the rest of us. He knows if Wayne and I are gone because he's a lot more aggressive when somebody comes, even toward people he knows well.

◇◇◇◇◇

I am sipping a cup of homemade cappuccino. This is the first winter I've been able to say I really enjoy cappuccino. I always thought it tasted like watered down instant coffee with a little milk added. I guess my taste buds are changing because I simply enjoy it now. I bought the ingredients to try the homemade, because good "boughten" is so expensive. I made a batch, tasted it, hmmm, not bad, but then added a small tin of my favorite boughten kind, and now this morning it tastes delicious. The bad part of it is the sugar content. That means it's got calories; I need to be ever mindful of those little things with big results.

Talking about calories, naturally thin women must have a lot less stress in their lives. Never having to think twice about what they eat, much less use 30 minutes of their day to go on a walk for exercise. You know what though? Walking is good for the naturally thin people too. It's good for the mind. I love to walk. Walking makes me feel so good.

◇◇◇◇◇

Karah, Emily, and Jolisa washed the dinner dishes, and I see there are five empty cans [jars] to take to the basement again. I know Jolisa took down three cans this morning. I think I do a lot of canning, but it doesn't take long at all to have a lot of empty cans in the basement again. I'm already looking forward to fresh garden produce. Winter move swiftly on!

◇◇◇◇◇

This winter I've taken time to do some craft/paint projects again, making signs for family and friends. I dream of having a work/retail shop here on the farm to craft and sell handcrafted items, but I am guessing our path is a little too untrod to make a go of it. Maybe though...I keep thinking about it.

◇◇◇◇◇

The three girls are again playing school. Jolisa has been having fun learning to read as a first-grader this year and then coming home and teaching her pupils. She's quite the teacher. By the time she has her

Bible memory verse memorized at the end of the week, the rest of us know it too. She's smaller than the rest of our children were at this age, but her enthusiasm makes up for her small stature.

For some reason, having food available for packing five lunch pails has been more of a challenge for me this year. I'm guessing some comes from the number five! The most I've ever had before was three. Five sandwiches take ten pieces of bread. Five bowls of fruit swipes a quart in a hurry. It cuts down a cake in a hurry too. And the cookie jars. We very seldom have chips or such snacks because it would take a bag a day. Sometimes I put in celery with peanut butter or something of the sort.

Today for lunch I made extra meatballs. The children like to wrap a meatball or two in foil, and then heat it at school for lunch. Wayne doesn't like something to heat, so he keeps eating cold sandwiches or wraps. I'd be sick and tired of them by now.

The schoolchildren don't want too many things in their lunches because it takes too much of their precious recess time to eat a lot. By the time they come home from school they are half starved, so it takes more food again. We have several picky eaters in the family. I am trying to teach them to eat whatever we prepare for them at the time, not just whatever suits their taste buds at that time. Why do we eat? To nourish our temples of God or because something tastes good? For nourishment. I try to keep that in mind, but my selfish desires are fighting to be known also.

Jolisa is telling me it is time to wash her hair. She and Jesse are the only ones who still need my help to do so. They grow up so fast, and I want to treasure each step of the way. Sometimes I find out some very interesting things while we are washing hair. Peering into their sweet faces and conversing one-on-one is priceless. Thank you, Lord, for every good thing.

◇◇◇◇◇

February 1, and everybody had been predicting a ferocious snowstorm. It should hit us today, they say. Probably around 5:00 PM. At

2:00, Wayne, Colleen, Jesse, and I went to Goshen to do some business. It hadn't started snowing yet. I was afraid the stores would be bombarded with shoppers trying to stock their pantries yet before the blast begins, but the stores we were in weren't bad at all. While we were in the last store, Wayne told me it was beginning to snow. And snow it did. That was probably around 4:00. On the way back we could sometimes barely see more than 100 feet in front of us. I was glad once we were safely home. Our house was freezing cold—or so it felt. With the wind blowing strong from the northeast, it hits the oldest, coldest part of our house. We stoked the coal stove, turned up the gas stove, and put on more layers of clothes.

Wayne and Brian fed the heifers, horses, and Sam the big spoiled dog. The girls and I cleaned up the house and made supper. Colleen made chili and sloppy joes. That helped warm us from the inside out. Meanwhile, it was seriously snowing and blowing. The schoolchildren were already rejoicing. They were pretty sure they wouldn't need to go to school in the morning.

I went to our east porch door to look out, and without opening the door I got snowed on. That strong, cold wind had a mind to enter wherever it wanted. Enter it did. I took a bunch of napkins and stuffed it into the cracks as well as I could. Wayne then wanted to look east before he went to bed. He looked out that door window, and still felt the snow blowing through the cracks, so he stuffed another rag into the cracks.

◇◇◇◇◇

We had a grand evening. We munched on popcorn, sipped on grape juice, played a game that got our blood pumping and the air moving throughout the house. It took a while to get everyone to bed because the girls decided they needed sweatpants, sweaters, and socks to survive. I didn't discourage them. By the time I went to bed, it was sleeting. I couldn't figure that one out because it was so cold. I prayed for everyone's safety and promptly fell asleep.

◇◇◇◇◇

On February 2, Wayne got up at 4:00 AM and checked things out. I woke up to the sound of the skid loader pushing snow. It was the time I usually get up, so I forced myself out of bed to put the coffee on. I watched Wayne push some snow and immediately doubted anybody with a healthy mind would try to traverse these roads this morning. Still, I decided I'd prepare Wayne's lunch bucket. Who knows? Men do think differently than women. I put the clean supper dishes away, finished a batch of yogurt, and tidied up here and there around the kitchen. All at once I heard that someone was stuck somewhere. The milkman, trying hard to do his job, was stuck at the corner a little east from here. Wayne went to help him with the skid loader. It actually didn't take long to get him going.

By then it was 5:00, and I had just snuggled up in front of the coal stove when Wayne came in. We both napped a while. Brian got up at 6:00 to do his chores. He also checked messages at the phone shack and came in saying there was no school. They all like school, but there is something special about having your school canceled for a day.

The children were all amazed as they came downstairs, proclaiming about the drifts of snow. This was definitely the biggest snowfall they had ever seen.

I made a brunch of pancakes, sausages, and eggs. Colleen did the laundry, and the little girls washed the dishes. Wayne, Brian, and Jesse went outside to push more snow and finish the chores. I had started two shirts for Brian, so I thought I'd finish those really quick, and then I'd put a quilt in frame. What a joke! I did finish those shirts, but not really fast.

I did have a very good day though. The girls decided they wanted to learn how to embroider, so we got out the needles, thread, transfers, ironing board, and the iron, and went to work. Emily embroidered a cute little duck with a lavender flower at its feet. Karah worked on a bear but didn't get it done as she also made her Aunt Leanna a birthday card. Jolisa used Crayola crayons that were made for transferring pictures on fabric. She did a picture of a little girl pushing her kitten around in a little cart. Jesse also started coloring a picture, but he was too easily distracted with all that snow. He spent most of the day outside.

You should've seen the kitchen! There was laundry hanging above the coal stove, my sewing machine, the little girls' projects, the newspaper, plus Wayne wanted smoothies at noon. Okay, that would be good since we're not making lunch anyway. He peeled three oranges, and when I left the kitchen those peelings were still on the counter. I peeled a banana, and we added some black and red raspberries, about 24 ounces of fresh homemade yogurt, blended it really well, and *mmmm*, that was delicious! Now we had those glasses on the table too. The children ate some crackers before they left the house, and I noticed those wrappers didn't all make it to the trash can either. Get the picture?

Brian, Jesse, and the three little girls left the house to go play in the snow. We have hills of it in the barnyard. We have a circle drive, and Wayne pushed most of the snow from the driveway onto the grass area in the middle. It made a wonderful playground. They also played with sleds. Sam, the spoiled dog, loved every minute of it. He ran and played just like the others. I think he thinks he's one of them!

Bless Colleen's heart. You can guess what her job was this afternoon. Yes, we all left the house, and she was left to do the cleaning. I know for a fact though that she was glad we all left—peace!

I hinted pretty loudly to my sister Ida, who lives across the driveway, that she could invite us for supper. She graciously agreed. She treated us to chicken, cheesy potatoes, and a salad—a corn-chip salad, which made our children cheer.

After supper Wayne wanted to go to the church hymn practice for the men. I decided the children and I would walk to visit a neighbor lady who has been laid up of sorts and spend the evening with her. Hopefully tomorrow we will have our regular routine back.

◇◇◇◇◇

February—the month of romance. It puts a smile on my face and a song in my heart. Who doesn't like to think about love...always remembering true love comes from God, and how blessed we have been.

Once upon a time, back in the late 1980s, I went to church with my sister Sue and her husband, Lavern. On the way to church, we passed this handsome fellow who was walking to church. In my premature, girlish mind I remember wondering if he would someday be my husband. We passed this fellow on CR 43, just north of CR 16. The interior of our buggy was a medium green. Church services were at Bill Bontragers. Some significant details tend to stick to my mind.

Several years later I was at my sister's house again for several days, and they were invited to one of their friends' house for supper one evening. The man of the house was a brother to *this fellow*. I did not care to stay at home alone, so I decided it would surely be safe to go along for the evening. We weren't there for long when *he* joined us. Oh misery! I wished I would have just stayed at home alone. It turned out to be safe though because he sure did not seem to notice me at all.

Another six months or so and I was at my sister Sue's house again. Lavern was building a silage bunker and had asked *him* to come help him for the day. He had on a dark-brown shirt, quite ugly for sure, but I still thought he was kind of cute. Not immature cute, but I admired his ways. He was almost four years older than I and a lot more mature. *He* sat on the west side of the kitchen table to eat lunch that day. I was on the east side. I remember I gave my nieces a lot of attention at the table because I really didn't want to look at *him* more than I had to. At least not when he knew I was looking. He didn't notice me anyway.

All at once *he* started coming around to the places where I was spending time with my friends. *He* even started talking to me. Finally he asked me out on a date—and that is when my life with Wayne began.

We could talk for hours—and still do. Communication is very important to both of us. One subject he always talked about was his desire to raise his family on a dairy farm. Inwardly I had to come to grips with that, hoping it would never mature. Wayne kept talking about it to me, and finally he had me just as enthused as he was. That's what love does! I ended up loving to dairy. Now our operation has changed again, but it has been okay.

Before we were married, my mom and dad's little dog did not like Wayne at all. Wayne tried his best to get on this dog's friendly side to no avail. The first time we came back to visit after our wedding, this dog decided he might as well like Wayne because he was friendly from then on.

As a young married wife, I sometimes struggled with coming up with enough different menu ideas. I made chicken-and-noodles and pancakes way too often. There came a time when I really didn't feel good in the mornings. Frying an egg and toast at 4:30 AM was torture. Finally it became torture for Wayne also because the eggs had extra protein in them. After crunching on an eggshell once too often, he volunteered to eat cereal for a while.

Colleen was born a little before our first anniversary, so Wayne volunteered to cook supper on our anniversary. We dined on toasted cheese sandwiches. I didn't mind. I was thankful he made us supper.

About the only time we have a hard time supporting each other is when we're sorting heifers. I don't imagine that will ever change. We manage not to eat each other up and we get the job done, but I never feel as dumb as when sorting heifers. Thankfully it doesn't happen often, and we remain to be best friends.

One day while hanging out the laundry, a trucker came to load up the last of the little steers. It kind of irked me that I had to leave my laundry, but I thought I had better go help him. I wished I would have known he was coming, so I could have prepared before he came. I emptied the laundry basket and then trotted out to help him. I ended up getting Colleen to help us, and we got the job done. Sometimes I wonder what stories these trucker guys have to tell about us women.

Wayne cleaned out the shed where these steers had been, and then later one day I went out and sprayed the walls, feed bunks, and water troughs with pure bleach to rid of any germs. Now that barn is full of heifers. The dairy barn is also full, so it takes a while to TMR-mix feed for all these, but Wayne loves doing it. We are thankful for this opportunity and already anticipate putting out the crops to feed again next winter.

Jesse is here beside me practicing writing his name. He's pretty tickled to be able to do it. He'll be glad once spring is here again, and he can go outside to lower his energy levels. He gets pretty bored with Colleen and me. During the day he often asks us when the schoolchildren are coming home from school. Several years ago I thought we'd never get to the point where the children could all dress themselves to go outside to play or do chores. Now we are there already. Sometimes Jesse needs help with his gloves, and I gladly help him with that.

February is the shortest month, but it feels like the longest to me. The holiday festivities are past; it's too cold to go out much. I ache to go on a long, warm walk, hang laundry outside in warm breezes, and eat fresh produce from the garden. I have to keep myself motivated even though I stay plenty busy with my motherly duties. This year I will try to stay focused on the joys of the coziness and closeness our house provides for us, even though it can sometimes be quite cold when the frigid north wind is blowing and the curtains sway a bit in the breeze.

◇◇◇◇◇

We'll enjoy our popcorn and grape juice, and Wayne and I our occasional Pepsi once the children are in bed. We read books and play marbles with the children. I guess February isn't so bad after all.

Year 4

Spring

I brewed myself a cup of Plantation Mint tea, and now I'm ready to sit and relax a while. The house is quiet, warm, and cozy. Wayne is home from work already, so he and Jesse are taking a nap. I enjoyed a bit of a siesta myself but nary for long. It did refresh me though. Even though Jesse is now five, he still takes a nap each day. If by chance he skips a day, like yesterday, he cries easily and doesn't enjoy the evening with the rest of the family. Last night he fell asleep on the recliner with me while he was waiting for Brian to shower. They always go to bed together. Jesse just could not stay awake any longer. I guess he is still the baby.

Even with the February blahs, I have really enjoyed this winter. Weather-wise it has been almost perfect. We've had gorgeous, sunny days bright with all the snow on the ground. It's beautiful being inside and looking out. The children have made plenty of snow angels and come in with wet clothes. I admire people's yards that are perfect, the snow left unblemished. Then I think of those rosy-cheeked, happy-faced children as they enjoy playing in the cold white stuff. I am glad for the way our yard looks. The children come in totally exhausted and wet, with sniffling noses and exciting stories of all they have been doing. We hang their dripping clothes on the drying rack above the coal stove. Usually by that time it's time to set the table for supper. No, I do not mind a messed-up yard. Our children are in a grand age.

One day I went to Spector's Dry Goods, a store in Shipshewana, to get some fabric we needed. They had this deal where if you spend $100, you get a $25 discount. Ella, one of the friendly ladies working there, pointed out that if I spent a few more dollars, I could get $25 more merchandise for free. Well, now I thought that would not be a wise decision to turn down a deal like that! I hadn't realized I was that close to the $100. All at once I could pick out a lot more than I had anticipated. I was tempted to get some fabric for myself but decided I'd better stick to really important choices. Although I do need dresses also, I knew the girls were in need of Sunday dresses. Besides, those are a lot more fun to sew.

The next Monday I decided to cut out all the clothes I had fabric for, so when I would get to the sewing machine I could just keep sewing. I didn't get all the cutting done because, well, that's just how Mondays are. "This and that" needed my attention too. I did cut Wayne a thick denim coat and a thin one, Colleen two dresses, Karah two dresses, Emily and Jolisa each a dress. Guess what? I did not have any waste fabric left when cutting the little girls' Sunday dresses. In fact, I couldn't make Jolisa's dress long-sleeved because I simply did not have enough fabric. She can use a short-sleeved summer dress too, but I had wanted the girls to all have the same Sunday dresses. I should have gotten a wee bit more fabric.

On the evening of my birthday, we had a chance to go to the Nappanee area, an Amish settlement 30 miles west of here, so we decided to spend the evening with some farmer friends. Our friend Lonnie also had a birthday that day, so we decided to order pizza for supper. Sarah made the best homemade ice cream I have tasted in a very long time. It reminded me of my mom's recipe. Turns out the recipes were very similar. It takes Rich's topping, Eagle Brand milk, and evaporated milk, so no wonder it tastes rich and creamy. We immensely enjoyed our evening.

◇◇◇◇◇

One Sunday close to my birthday, we spent the evening with three couples. The women and I all have birthdays on the same day. We have been getting together like this for five years or more. It is such a neat group. The eldest lady is in her 60s, two are in their 50s, and I have yet to hit 40. Age does not make a difference in our friendship. In fact, maybe it enhances it. We had a special time catching up on each other's lives. It was worth celebrating another birthday.

◇◇◇◇◇

When we got home that night, my dad came to the door and said the calves weren't where they are supposed to be. Oh groan. This was a frigidly cold evening. It was close to ten o'clock, high time to get the schoolchildren to bed. But those 60 calves, weighing 500 pounds each, had to be put into the barn. I hurriedly got our four little children tucked into bed, and then I bundled up thickly, except I couldn't find any thick gloves. I headed out to help Wayne and Brian. The stars were shining very brightly. It was a beautiful evening, but it was *cold* and time for bed. It was also very dark.

These calves were all congregated in a bunch close to the gate where we could chase them into the lane, to then head north toward the barn. Wayne had situated the skid loader close to the barn with the lights shining on the barn to give the calves a clue to where they were going. I don't know how much a calf can think, but it did help. With headlamps strapped to their heads, Wayne and Brian calmly tried to guide the calves out into the lane. They had me situated in the lane. I was to make sure they headed north. I'm guessing the lane is 40 feet wide, even though it might as well have been 80 feet. It was cold and pitch black. If Wayne wanted to give me instructions, like shaking the chain on the gate so the calves knew there was a gate there they could go through, I was blinded because of those headlamps. I told him *not* to look at me, and then we were fine. We talked calmly. There is no use getting these calves in a tizzy. Wayne and Brian had to work close to 20 minutes just to move the calves approximately 30 feet out into the lane.

You know me. I was praying that once they headed my way they'd go north. That's what they did. One calf went north into the field instead of going into the lane first, and by the time they got to the barn two more had slipped through the five-strand barbed-wire fence and joined it. We put the 57 in the barn. While I guarded those, Wayne and Brian got the other 3 in short order.

We discovered something must have made them stampede. They had gone through a new five-strand barbed-wire fence, breaking off five wooden posts. I guess why will remain a mystery.

We'd rearranged some gates to help guide the calves to the barn, so by the time we had those where they belonged and we were in the house, it was close to 11:00. During that time, Colleen had come home with her friends, so we needed to chat with her a while. Sleep was slow in coming for me. My heart rate isn't normally that high when I go to bed.

Last night as I was folding laundry, Jesse was slowly getting dressed to go outside. He looked at me with those big brown eyes of his and said, "Mom, do you know what I would do with a monster?"

He was quite serious.

"No," I said. "What would you do?"

"Well, I'd use a corn whacker and whack off his head!"

I asked him what a monster was. He said it was a big animal. I just wondered, I told him. He said he thinks they are probably there where those big, changing lights are, meaning the northern lights. We saw the northern lights this winter, and they must have been spooky to him.

One dreary, rainy day a robin was in a tree outside our porch window cheerily singing to his Master. I was at the sewing machine busily sewing on dresses, and Jesse was playing on the floor close beside me. We talked about the fact that the sun has not been shining through the clouds the last few days. It was plain drab, with plenty of mud to accompany it. Yet that robin kept right on singing loudly and cheerily. He didn't care if the sun was shining or not. He totally trusted his Master. I told Jesse I wanted to be more like that robin. Totally trusting, totally cheerful...we serve the same Master!

◇◇◇◇◇

One night while we were eating supper I mentioned I had a nagging headache, and I was tight between my shoulder blades. Wayne wondered what the problem was, as I really didn't have a stressful day. I said it comes from sitting so tense at our school district's spelling bee.

Jolisa, sitting beside me, looked up at me quizzically and questioned, "Tents? Were you all sitting in tents today?" It was too cute not to laugh, but we quickly explained to her what "sitting tense" means.

I immensely enjoyed the afternoon at the spelling bee. There were more than 70 eighth-graders participating. As the district chairman said, it's totally amazing what the human mind can do if it decides to. These kids could confidently spell words they could hardly pronounce, let alone use in their daily vocabulary. They all did a super job.

◇◇◇◇◇

This past winter I experienced another day of feeling tense. I hosted a Pampered Chef cooking party. One thing understood: I am *not* a party person. I don't mind going to one every once in a while, but not hosting one. So why did I plan one? Well, I do love their products, and I always bake our pizza on their stoneware pans. I broke two of them one night while getting them out of the pantry to make pizza for supper.

The next week I received flyers in the mail showing me what the host specials were for the next two months. What a coincidence—not really, because I'd happened to see a consultant in church the day after I broke the pans, and I of course told her what happened. So, after consulting with Wayne, I took the plunge and booked a party.

I put a quilt in frame and told some of the ladies they could stay to help quilt after the party, thus I could kill two birds with one stone. With nine ladies from different parts of the community sitting in my kitchen, I told the consultant we needed to have introductions as not everybody likes each other. I caught my mistake as soon as it left my tongue, but it was too late! I could not swallow it. What an uproar that caused. It was an icebreaker. I immensely enjoyed the day. I've also really appreciated the many new products I was able to get. We've used them close to every day since getting them. How did I survive without these products?

Men, if you want to impress your wife for whatever reason, buy them Pampered Chef products. They'll love you, and you'll love the food she now enjoys cooking.

The quilt I put in frame was one Colleen had pieced last winter using fabric we inherited from Mom's quilt shop. It is just a simple squares pattern in shades of blue. The blues have little pink flowers in it, making it look cheerily feminine. It took me several weeks to get it quilted. I didn't work on it every day, just mostly in the afternoon for an hour or two. Now that it is quilted, I need to bind it yet, and then I'll be relieved to have it completed. I really enjoy piecing and quilting quilts, but if I have other duties beckoning, I hardly have the patience it takes.

I started learning to quilt before I went to school. With a quilt shop attached to our house, it was almost as natural as breathing. I already see the next generation not as enthused about it, but I do plan on teaching my daughters how to quilt and appreciate the art.

◇◇◇◇◇

My sister Ida had water in her basement resulting from all the rain we've had recently. One day she heard someone down in her basement, and upon checking, she found Jesse sitting on the bottom steps fishing. He didn't catch anything that day, except I do believe he snagged his aunt's heart.

◇◇◇◇◇

On Saturday I left the weekly cleaning to the four girls, and I did more laundry. Colleen had done the laundry three times already this week, but I decided to wash the good coats, sweaters, and then also all I could gather up of regular laundry.

By the time I was done hanging out the clothes, Jesse came from the barn telling me Daddy wants help vaccinating heifers. He and Brian still had 30 to do, and it just works better if there are three of us. We had several minor stresses, but we got them all done none worse for the wear.

By the time I got to the house, it was soon after 10:00. The girls had the cleaning pretty well done by then, so I made lunch. I made mashed potatoes, chicken dressing that I had frozen earlier, hamburger gravy, and green beans. Chocolate chip cookies baked on stoneware rounded out the meal. The children thought we had a grand meal.

The rest of the day was spent doing odds and ends. Wayne fixed a broken tile, cleaned the barns, and mixed feed for the cattle, preparing for Sunday.

In a few weeks, Brian will graduate from eighth grade, thus ending his formal education. He will be a big asset here on the farm this summer by doing a lot of the field work. I appreciate his willing hands here at home. You know mothers' concerned ways when we see our young boys hitching up big work horses and heading to the fields. He tells me not to worry; he knows what he is doing. I know. I do need to trust, but accidents do happen. Lord be with us as we go about our work.

My favorite time of year is coming up...summer! Fresh garden produce and s'mores over the fire. Going on my two-mile walk with one, two, three, or four little ones biking along. Listening to the birds sing. Being free of coats, boots, scarves, and the coal stove. Jumping on the trampoline with the children until we're all red-faced and hot. Running races and showing the children this mama can still run. Going to some friend's house for the evening and coming home before dark. I know I have to work harder in the summer, but I love feeling physically fit, and warm, and in the evening being tired to the bone.

◇◇◇◇◇

We have been enjoying beautiful weather. Wonderful, warm, sunny, almost-summer weather. I love it to the max. I am actually thawed out. No more wearing a jacket all day long. Yes, we all love this time of year here on the farm. Dirty toes, smelly farm clothes, lots of laundry to wash, but at least no more thick, dark girls' socks to launder and sort. No more blaming of the other sisters for stealing the other's socks. Those socks can just have a long rest this summer. We don't mind having a lot of laundry in the summer, not with hanging them out and then bringing them in nice and fluffy. That is if the wind is from the right direction.

One thing I do not enjoy in the summer is the dust on our dirt road. And you know we practically live on the road. Just this week the county road guys hauled load after load of the ugliest, stoniest, brown gravel on our road. They got half of our mile done in a day, now today they are flying past here with load after load to finish the rest of the stretch. Guess which way the wind is blowing? It is awful. There are several ladies in the neighborhood who feel like running after the trucks and telling them like it is, but…sigh…is this where nonresistance comes in? I feel like putting a sign out by the road reading "Eat Your Own Dust!" I know that is not Christlike at all, so Lord, grant me patience without grumbling.

I've been trying to get Wayne and Brian to shoot sparrows for me. I wish I had a big enough gun that I could pepper them. Well, we do have a big enough gun, but it's too big for me to handle. The BB gun that I can handle is not powerful enough to even scare them out of the tree. My men are too busy in the fields to think about Mom's wants. Noisy sparrows work on my nerves. Jesse told me I shouldn't shoot the overeater birds. No, Jesse, I would not shoot the red-winged blackbirds, just the sparrows. We have this joke about the red-winged blackbirds calling "overeater" to me as I go on a walk, but then on the way back they are calling, "Looking sweeter!"

Talking about little guys reminds me of my nephew Jeryl, who will be six in July. One day he was sitting on their kitchen counter, staring out the window, deep in thought. At once he said, "Mom, it just seems like I am married." Whatever would bring on a thought like that? his mom asked. He didn't know.

In March we butchered the three little pigs. They are some good eating. One of them we cut into six pieces, put in several garbage bags, and put them in the freezer. I have some big plans for that little runt. I want to soak it in a marinade and then grill it on the charcoal grill. That should make for some lip-smacking, tender eating.

I've already invited someone for half of the piggy. They came and helped us get the three piggies in the freezer, so I'm thinking they deserve to help us enjoy them too. Esther can bake the softest, the most delicious cinnamon rolls. Do I dare ask her to bring those for dessert? Absolutely! My children will cheer.

Dessert brings to mind my flop of a dessert I made recently. My sister Ida had invited a couple from church for supper one Sunday night. She asked if I could bring dessert. We had a very busy weekend with friends here from out of state, so every minute detail had to be thought out beforehand, and everything had to be organized so I could get everything done. I had planned to make an easy dessert on Saturday afternoon after coming home from a sale and before getting ready for company for supper. Before I go on, do not be stressed out for me because I was enjoying every minute of this weekend. We love when our friends come, and we weren't disappointed this time either. We had a blast.

On with the dessert. I had decided on French éclair dessert. When I was ready to begin, I discovered I didn't have enough instant vanilla pudding. I trotted across the driveway to sister Ida and asked to borrow some. She didn't have any either, but she did have instant white chocolate pudding that I decided was good enough. Next on the ingredient list was Cool Whip. I dislike the flavor of Cool Whip so I always use Rich's topping. I had some Rich's topping that was mixed with powdered sugar and cream cheese in the refrigerator that should have been used, so I decided to use that plus add more Rich's topping to get the desired amount. I lined the 9 x 13 Tupperware with graham crackers, dumped some pudding on them, smoothed it out a bit, added another layer of crackers, dumped more pudding on them, smoothed it out, and added another layer of crackers. Luckily I had enough. Now the recipe asked for a chocolate topping made of butter, sugar, and cocoa, but I wanted more chocolate—real chocolate. I have a recipe asking for chocolate baking squares, but of course I don't have any of those. We love the chocolate topping on the Swiss Roll Cake, so the cook that I am, I decided to use that recipe but double it for the 9 x 13. (The Swiss Roll Cake is created in a jelly roll pan.) My concoction looked good.

Sunday night we enjoyed a roast turkey supper. Bring on the dessert! I got a serving spoon to put into the pan, and that layer of thick chocolate was so hard I should've used an ice pick to break it apart. We had a major fit of the giggles. How embarrassing, but it was good. If you like chocolate as much as I do, anyway. Wayne thought it was too sweet, and he got a stomachache. I don't think it was entirely from the dessert. The next day while nobody was looking I picked off the leftover chocolate and ate it like a candy bar. Then I walked two miles.

We enjoy watching two healthy, fast-growing workhorse colts enjoying the warmer weather with their mamas in the small field west of the house. One colt gave me fits the first day of his life. Wayne checked the barn before he went to work that morning, and, yes, Lou had her baby. A big boy. When Brian went to do his chores, he soon came back in asking if I would please come help get the big guy up because it is really important they eat soon after birth, and it was obvious that this one hadn't. We tried and tried, and finally it was time Brian went to school, so I decided to ask a neighbor man for help. He helped a little, gave the mare a shot of oxytocin, as it appeared she couldn't let her milk down. I made several phone calls asking for advice, and then I came back and worked with the mare and colt. I'd milk on my hand and put the really thick colostrum in the colt's mouth. Then I tried to get the colt interested again. Newborn colts aren't the smartest creatures in the world. I was elated and in awe once the colt did actually take hold and eat! Please keep in mind that I am scared stiff of those huge horses. I love driving draft horses, but I am far enough away from them then. The mama stayed calm as long as I kept feed and hay there for her. I only had to exit by way of the side of the stall once because the mare turned and her hind end was too close to the door for comfort for me. I didn't get accomplished what I had in mind to do that day, but I did feel like I had accomplished something.

Year 4

Summer

After eating a big noon meal of mashed potatoes, gravy, peas, grilled BBQ meatballs, and a grand finale of baked cream pie, I am stuffed and ready for the recliner. But, alas, I am not that lucky. This happens to be a Saturday. A gorgeous, 70-degree, lazy breeze, awesome kind of summer day. I am rejoicing that so far it has been a very normal day. Not just thankful—more like thankful from the depths of my heart kind of thankful. Lately we have had some stark reminders to really be thankful for our ho-hum kind of days. We never know when the Lord has a big change of plans for us.

This morning after Wayne and Brian had a breakfast of fried potatoes and tomato gravy, and I had my banana, yogurt, and granola medley, our day began in earnest. Wayne and Brian got the six horses hitched, and Brian headed to the field to finish up the plowing. They are pretty well on schedule this year. Brian has done a lot of the field work while Wayne was at work. That has been a major plus.

After a cold, wet spring, it has now been dry enough to get a lot done in the fields. For those of us living here on this heavy clay soil, this week has been a blessing in getting the field work done. If the weather holds out, they hope to get the planting done this next week.

I let the four youngest sleep a while longer while I washed the dishes from breakfast and last night's popcorn, iced tea, and pop party. I cleaned the kitchen counters, shined the outside of the fridge and stove, scrubbed the sinks and toilet, dusted the furniture, and watered the houseplants. By that time the children were awake and getting used to the fact that their mom now wants some of their precious time. Usually they are very involved in our weekly cleaning, but I kind of liked the idea of having some quiet time all to myself.

They were still lucky enough to have things to do to help me out the rest of the day. Karah emptied the stairway and swept the upstairs hallway and stairs. She watered Colleen's plant upstairs and did numerous other odd jobs. Emily washed the door windows and mirrors, swept the living room area rug so I could put the furniture on it, making it easier to sweep and mop the floor. Jolisa took the throw rugs outside to shake off the dirt and hang them over the porch railing to air out a while. I then let them play a while as I swept and mopped the floors.

While the floor was drying, we cleaned up outside, trimming along the walks and sweeping and washing off the walkway. That trimming job took me back to my childhood because we had to use the shears today to do the trimming. Our weed-eater needs to go to the fix-it shop. The girls helped me, and it was okay. It just took more time. I remember trimming was a longsome job before and how we rejoiced when we finally got a weed-eater. Sure wish that they'd be a tad more people-friendly. Usually it gives me the fits getting it started or else the string doesn't want to cooperate.

Anyway, the girls took the trash out to be burned, I repotted a fern, and somehow the time slipped away from us. Suddenly I realized it was high time to get lunch made. The men do not like their noon break wasted on waiting for lunch, so we needed to hurry. I quickly dashed to the basement for potatoes and then filled the pot with water to heat to get a head start while I peeled the potatoes. In the meantime, Karah lit the gas grill and helped me mix and shape meatballs that she then grilled and slathered with BBQ sauce. Emily made a salad. Jolisa set the table and ran errands for Karah at the grill. All went well, and I don't think the men waited more than a minute or two.

I like to make a full-course meal like that on Saturdays, especially since Wayne has a day job off the farm. That's a special time to all sit down together for a meal. Sure, we eat together in the evenings too, but I hardly ever make mashed potatoes and the works for supper. I prefer lighter suppers. If I cooked mashed potatoes all the time, I'd have to walk four miles daily instead of the normal two.

I transplanted the asparagus patch this spring with hopes of enlarging the patch because we never have enough to satisfy everybody. I sent one of the children to dig up the roots, but she was soon back saying she couldn't dig them out. *Oh come on,* I thought. She must not be trying hard enough.

I suggested to Wayne to take the skid loader and dig them out, but he thought surely I could just dig them out with the shovel. I couldn't either. Wayne tried with the shovel too, and he couldn't. So he went and put the forks on the skid loader and finally got out those roots. We were in for a big surprise. I'm guessing those roots were three feet deep.

Wayne moved them to the west garden where we had dug a trench to put them in. We then covered them with a generous layer of calf manure and straw. Once it started to warm up, we had hopes that they would grow. We watched pretty closely. The patch is beside the path that leads to our phone shack, so each time we walk by on our way to use the phone we check to see if we can find new shoots. We made a funny sight one evening when most of us were kneeling beside the patch to see how many new shoots we could find. Once we had several, I made soup with those.

Asparagus Soup

Asparagus soup is really simple to make. I sauté the chopped asparagus and some chopped onions in butter, thicken with a bit of flour, and add some milk and water. I add salt, pepper, and some cheese if I desire. It's ready for the table.

◇◇◇◇◇

A gully washer of a rainstorm just came up, and Brian got majorly soaked. It's coming down hard. I can't see quite clearly, but it appears he only had several rounds to plow to finish up. Should have been a half hour earlier this morning or when they went back out this afternoon. Oh well, could have been worse.

Jolisa smashed a thumb while closing the windows in a hurry. Ouch! Now she has another excuse when it comes to dish-washing time.

"Mom, I need to be here Monday night to play this, and I need to be there Friday night to play that, and we friends want to go shopping on Wednesday night..." That's the story around here this summer with a 16-year-old living in the house. I'm not complaining, but it is something to get used to. I depend heavily on Colleen when she's home, and it looks like it is slipping from my hands as she has plans to start working at a local bakery. I had a hard time adjusting to the fact, but I know it will be a good experience for her. I am thankful she has the opportunity to work in a Christian atmosphere. I will need to step up again and work at a brisker pace, and the three younger girls will have more learning experiences, which will be good for us all. I hope.

We don't need to water our seedlings tonight. It is still raining hard. This rain should make the things in the garden grow. The radishes were up in three days. We'll be eyeing those too. I need to plant melons and potatoes yet. Maybe a bit more corn if space allows. Usually I freeze around 90 quarts of corn, but I won't this year. We still have a lot in the freezer. I guess we got kind of tired of it and ate more peas this last year.

The rhubarb is really nice this year, and I finally have enough of our own. I baked a rhubarb cake, and now I promised Wayne I'd make him a pie next week. I also want to make rhubarb torte for him yet, and then maybe I'll try my hand at some jam or else some juice. I like it thickened with some Jell-O, and then I eat it with cottage cheese, but really, rhubarb is easy on my diet. I can easily pass on those dishes. For Wayne's sake I keep trying to like it. Maybe someday.

This spring we were invited to my sister Leanna and her husband's place for Sunday dinner, and she made dandelion gravy. That was new for us. I'd never tasted it before. I liked it okay, as did Wayne, but my honest opinion? The bacon and ham make the gravy. I could hardly taste the dandelion greens. It was fun, anyway. Leanna and I taught our children to talk in "pig Latin" that day. I'm not too sure that was a good idea because they sometimes drive me crazy now with their chattering. Keeps life interesting.

◇◇◇◇◇

I've heard a lot of people say they didn't get the strawberries this spring as they had anticipated. Some of us came to the conclusion it's because the plants did not get the sunshine they needed while they were blooming. We had a wet, dreary spring, with very few sunny days while the strawberries were in bloom. We got enough to eat fresh, and I need to be satisfied with that. I saw in town a five-quart pail of freshly picked strawberries was priced over $14. Too much for me to pay, but I know if I'd be in the picking end of the deal, I'd want a good price too. Strawberries are a lot of work.

One of my absolute favorite food combinations is vanilla ice cream and fresh strawberries. I'd love to fall into a big bowl full of that and eat my way out. I used to crave chocolate cake with it too, but that has gotten too sweet for me. I'm glad because I don't need those calories.

I've also learned to like strawberry shortcake. My siblings and I didn't grow up with that dish as Wayne's family did. Several of the children really like it too, and I suspect with time the rest will too.

Fresh garden lettuce sandwiches are on the menu tonight, along with strawberry shortcake. We eat a lot of radishes and green onions too. One of my sisters-in-law gave me a salad spinner to try out, and I've decided it's a must for garden lettuce. It does save time drying that lettuce. It is really important to get all those crunchies off the lettuce or my family is turning up their noses. (Crunchies are specks of garden dirt.)

Karah and I planted the keeper potatoes the second week in June on a hot, humid day. We made row markers with the seeder, put the potatoes on top, and covered the whole area with straw. Now, it'll be interesting to see what size of crop we will get. Hopefully we'll have better luck then we did last year.

The red potato plants look like a picture. I've only sprayed them once for bugs, plus I put fish fertilizer in the sprayer too. We use an organic bug spray for potatoes, tomatoes, cabbage, broccoli—actually just about any fruits and vegetables. I had bugs on the tomato plants too, but the spray seemed to take care of those in a hurry.

The children and I mulched a lot of the garden with straw. The soil needs the organic matter, plus I thought it would lessen the weeding this summer. We're not getting lazy, but who doesn't want a break every once in a while? I love to open the west porch shades in the morning and look out at the garden. I let my mind wander to God and his many, many blessings. What an awesome privilege I have living here in the country surrounded by nature and all these people I so dearly love.

This is the first summer we have been able to keep Baltimore orioles here. They usually just pass through in the spring. This year Brian built a feeder, and we put black raspberry jam out that was crystallized anyway, hoping the orioles would like it. It appears that they do enjoy it.

The feeder is in the flowerbed right outside the east living room windows. The other morning I was sitting on my dilapidated recliner trying to wake up and get my mind focused on the day ahead, when I heard a peculiar loud chatter at the window. It sounded quite earnest. Upon investigating, I saw an oriole perched on the window screen, seemingly trying to tell me something. Then he flew to the next window screen and did the same thing, before flying to perch on the tree. I promptly went out and filled the empty jelly jar. That oriole made my day.

◇◇◇◇◇

We were happy to have gorgeous weather to put up the first-cutting hay. Wayne and Brian chopped 10 acres and filled a forage bag. Then they round-baled 10 acres. I got lucky enough to drive the team to bring up the bales. It was warm and gorgeous. Then a day later we had a nice, slow rain. I imagined the hayfields soaking up that beautiful rain. The first cornfield did not fare so well. Right after Wayne had planted that field, we had a lot of rain and the ground got too hard. Brian ripped up that field again, and Wayne replanted it. One of our neighbors had to do the same thing. It takes lots and lots of patience to farm, but for some reason we still love it.

Yesterday Emily had an appointment at the eye doctor in Shipshewana, so I was gone most of the day. Now today we went to a discount eyeglass place in Topeka to order her glasses, also stopping to buy fabric to sew clothes for the children. It took a wad, but I figured with what I saved by getting the discount eyeglasses, I could get fabric for three pairs of pants, four dresses, and the notions it takes, plus have money left over. It worked on my nerves to spend so much time on the road—14-miles round trip both days, but I thought I had to squeeze the most out of our dollars.

Colleen now works at the Rise and Roll Bakery four days a week. She likes her job even if she has to get up at 3:30 in the morning. It's a good experience for her and the rest of us too. I miss our time to talk the most. I am thankful for the days that she is home, but lately it seemed those days I wasn't at home.

I decided I must cut out all the clothes this afternoon from the fabric I bought this forenoon so I can sew every slip chance I can get. The girls need the dresses for school, and I must stay at it. All too soon school will start again. The sewing machine has been dormant, but some way, somehow, that must change. I much prefer gardening and enjoying the great outdoors in the summer, but motherly duties call. I'll enjoy the sewing too, once I get to it.

Golden cobs of corn dripping in butter and salt grace our table these days. Munching on corn-on-the-cob with a family of eight is fun. Everybody sounds the same, and we can just eat to our hearts' content! Frying some bacon and then adding all the garden goodies, plus some sausage, to make a stew is a wonderful one-pot meal we all love this time of the year. It is healthy, and I can eat gobs and gobs of it and not gain an ounce. One drawback, though, is the time it takes to get this food from the garden to the table. But you know what? It is economical, educational—simplicity at its finest—and an awesome privilege to have from our heavenly Father.

We had never taken a family vacation with our six children, but for three days in July we splurged and went to Holmes County, Ohio, to visit some friends. We filled a treasure box deep in our hearts with wonderful memories. Warm circles prance around our hearts when we reminisce, which we do quite frequently. The Holmes County scenery, to say the least, is beautiful.

Thursday afternoon, upon entering Holmes County, we stopped at several friends' places to chat a bit. At one place we were treated to some delicious black raspberry Danish pastry and lemonade.

We then traveled to the Andy Weaver and Michael Miller farm, where we have special ties. We are deeply connected with losing our moms the same year from similar health issues. Our families have many similarities. We enjoyed an evening of walking around their rolling dairy and chicken farm. Then we retired around the campfire and enjoyed s'mores and donuts we'd taken along from the bakery Colleen works at.

Jesse has some smashing memories from his stay in Holmes County. While riding a bike, as little five-year-old boys love to do, he took a flying ride down the hill, lost control, did a somersault, and skinned his elbow. It cost a few tears. He's not used to riding a bike on hills. In the wee hours of the night, I heard a thud and flew out of bed to investigate. I found Brian and Jesse coming down the hallway toward the bedroom they were staying in. Jesse was crying, and Brian was proclaiming what a big baby he was as only big brothers can. Jesse had been thirsty, and Brian thought it not necessary to get up at that time of the night, but he did take him to the bathroom to get a drink. They didn't have a flashlight with them, and it being an unfamiliar house, Jesse turned too soon to go back down the hallway. He flipped down the stairs, crashing into the closed door. Poor little guy; I pitied him so. He could have had a bad injury, but luckily he was okay.

On Friday, Michael and some more friends, the Daniel Millers, gave us a grand tour of their community. I loved seeing the old homesteads on winding country roads. In the evening we were loaded onto a flatbed wagon to be entrusted to our young friend Brandon's tractor driving skills on those domineering hills of theirs. We joined a group of about 30 people on top of one of these hills for a picnic. I don't know which was best—their delicious supper that was set up looking like it belonged on a magazine page, the fabulous view, or the wonderful fellowship. Combine the three, plus the fun our children had with their new friends, mix it all together and just imagine. I thanked the Lord for connecting us.

Saturday we spent the day at Michael and Rhoda's farm, visiting with more friends, eating, going on another hayride, and simply enjoying the day. Our farm boys swam in the muddy farm pond created by a little dam. Sometimes the only clean things on them were their eyeballs.

Alas, all good things must come to an end. We started for home around 4:00 PM. I couldn't even stay awake for more than 30 miles. One tired, but happy bunch came home around 9:30. Sam was overjoyed to see us. He's one spoiled dog.

◇◇◇◇◇

Sunday evening several neighbors came to hear about our trip. We sat in the shade on the east side of the house, close to the road, talking, eating popcorn, and drinking ice water trying to stay cool. A vehicle sped by from the east with one of the passengers barking like a ferocious dog. Naturally Sam chased the intruder. We yelled at him to get back, and just like that another vehicle flew from the west and caught him unaware. Too late! What a horrible scene! Please believe me, I in no way compare Sam's life to a human's, but it was still awful. I cannot imagine how one feels to see a human being hit or hurt otherwise. I am so sorry, and I pray that if you have witnessed such an accident, the Lord will erase that picture from your mind.

Even though Sam was just a dog, he was a part of our family and somehow snuck deep into our hearts. He survived the impact and seems to be improving. The children spend a lot of time with him as he's recovering. He can easily communicate. We usually know what he wants. I know dogs are just dogs, but their loyalty to loved ones sometimes surpasses humans'. I remember my mom saying when her dad died, upon returning home from the hospital, my grandmother told the dog, who was lying by the sidewalk, that it was now all past, and the dog had tears rolling down his face.

Through this ordeal with Sam, my sister Sue said they had a stray that needed a home. The dog needs children to play with, and they think she's the dog for us. The girls desperately want the dog, and Brian just as strongly does not want it. He's afraid the girls will not give Sam the attention he needs to get better, plus Sam might feel betrayed. But the girls say their hearts are big enough for two dogs. Who will win? Daddy says the girls win. The girls say Brian will fall in love with the new dog. The little girls say her name will be Mandy. Colleen says she has to see and spend time with her before we can name her. What does this mama say? I choose to stay out of it because I really don't relish the thought of two dogs, especially one still in the puppy stage. I know a lot of the training will fall on my shoulders because I'm the one who's home all the time. So I left the decision up to Wayne and will try to be satisfied.

◇◇◇◇◇

We have been happy with the nice hay we were able to put up for the first and second cuttings. While walking through the fields to pick black raspberries, I noticed the next cutting looks really nice too. Next on the list is corn harvest—a busy time of the year but very satisfying.

I will definitely miss the little girls helping when they're back in school. They can make a lot of steps for me, especially during canning season. This year Karah is in fifth grade, Emily in third grade, and Jolisa in second grade. With Wayne and Colleen working off the farm, it'll be me and the boys at home during the forenoon. I will enjoy that too. I hope I can fully grasp the golden opportunity this is.

Fall

This has definitely been the summer of the dogs. The dog days of summer were warm, really warm, and I loved it. My fingers and toes were even warm.

Our faithful friend Sam that got hit on the road died a week and a half after the accident. I think the birds on our farm even mourned. I know we all did. He was quite the dog.

That stray terrier dog that Colleen brought home is quite the dog too. She's downright ugly and messes in our mudroom every night. (Wayne's dogs have to sleep in there.) Yet some of us kind of like her. I don't want to keep her, as she works on my nerves, yet she is kind of sweet. We all named her Mandy. The flowers here by the house are the only ones that grow nice on the whole place, as the rest of the flower beds are thick with tree roots, but now Mandy digs around in these nice ones, breaking off and squashing down the flowers. They're not nice anymore, plus the walks are always dirty from her messes.

I can't blame it all on Mandy because we do have another Lab-mix pup. This one is black and already big for his two months of age. A neighbor boy came across this one, brought him home, and we bought him. We were tickled pink. Then the arguments began in earnest. What shall we name this dog?

I wanted to name him Ben. A big, black Lab dog needs a masculine name, not some sort of Tippy, Frisky, or Buddy sort of name. Nobody seemed to agree with my choice. The name choices flew wildly around the house—and always a negative response echoed from somewhere. Someway, somehow "Jacob" stuck. Now he goes by Jacob, and sometimes I hear Jake. That's okay with me. Now, if only he'd stay out of the flower beds and not mess in the mudroom. The mudroom is actually cleaner than normal because after the men dispose of the offenses, I scrub it down with strong soap water. Hopefully the dogs will be potty trained soon. I do like a good dog. I just wish they'd come already trained, all grown up, and melded into the family. I'm never that lucky. Colleen, a major dog lover, still dreams of owning a Yorkie. Upon coming home from work she always stops to give the dogs some attention before coming into the house. Yorkies are pretty expensive, so I doubt her dream will ever come true.

The heat of this summer, plus the nice rains we received, was good for the crops through this area. There are beautiful fields of corn and hay. I noticed a lot of oats were harvested too. I also saw some really poor fields. One of ours that was planted, and then we got a lot of rain, just had a hard time of it.

This summer was so beautiful weather-wise. I enjoy spending time outside working in the garden, the yard, and helping in the hayfield. It was just simply nice to be outside, but it was all dampened by the turbulent times we live in. There were many deaths among our people. That is from God. Then there are so many leaving our faith searching for something better. Where can we find peace in broken promises?

Wayne and I were to Iowa to a funeral of a friend who was attacked by a bull. She died three days after the attack. Such a sad accident. Many, many people traveled many miles to show their love. To see over 1100 people gathered in one big circle, surrounding the family of nine children, four in-laws, the husband, and two grandchildren was overwhelming. The love of God is still pulling us together and ever closer to him. I ached for the family. I know what it is like to say goodbye to your mom, and yet I know peace in accepting God's will. It's not always easy, but we are promised we will not go this road alone. The Lord is with us.

In the sermon at the funeral, one of the ministers came across the topic of the prodigal son. I was so agreed, and he illustrated it in such an interesting fashion. If you look up the word "prodigal" in the dictionary, it tells you: 1) Addicted to wasteful expenditure, as of money, time, or strength; extravagant. 2) Yielding in profusion; bountiful. 3) Lavish; profuse. One who is wasteful or profligate; a spendthrift. (A "profligate" is lost or insensible to principle, virtue, or decency, a reckless spendthrift, recklessly extravagant.)

I found it necessary to examine myself. Do I have anything in my house, our farm, our clothes, and our mode of transportation that is extravagant? How much money do I spend on things not necessary because I want things to look nice? How many dishes of food do I prepare that are too lavish and not just for the healthy nourishment of our bodies? How much money do we spend on a fancy horse and buggy to be noticed by others? Do we have more clothes than we really need? Is our house in the latest fashion? The list could go on and on. Moderation, moderation, moderation.

Duties continue to call. This week I baked a double-batch of pumpkin whoopee pies. Poof, those were gone! I'd also doubled the frosting recipe and had a lot left over. Now this morning Brian suggested I bake Little Debbie cookies and use the leftover frosting. I thought it was a good suggestion. I think I will appease him. He needs to till the garden for me today, so he will be hungry as always. I can't imagine having several adolescent boys to feed and clothe. It would be interesting, though.

There are dishes to put away, peaches to peel, ironing to do, tomatoes and cucumbers to bring in from the garden, dresses to lengthen for Karah, Emily, and Jolisa. The list goes on from one day to the next. I love my calling.

Karah, Emily, and Jolisa have been on a card-making frenzy. They spend a lot of time at the table on our porch cutting, pasting, stamping, and conversing. They dream of having a card-making business. They actually did get to sell some, thanks to grandparents, aunts, and friends. I remember as a young girl dreaming of making and selling all kinds of things. Some of these dreams actually materialized and proved to be profitable. Lemonade sales were my first business. Busloads of tourists would come to my grandmother's quilt shop, and I'm guessing some people drank lemonade who didn't even like it. Who could refuse a chubby, dimple-cheeked little girl's lemonade all the way out in the country with no other customers in sight? It was fun.

◇◇◇◇◇

You should hear Jolisa and Jesse having a major giggling fit while tearing around the house. Jolisa is lying on her tummy on an old throw blanket, arms outstretched, hanging on to an upside down barstool that Jesse is using to pull her around the house. Around and around the circle consisting of the living room, kitchen, and porch they go. The noise level could stand downgrading several decibels, but I've decided to let them have fun. The blanket is worn anyway and the floor is clean, so they can giggle to their hearts' content.

Karah is at the table on the porch crafting unique greeting cards, which she loves doing.

Emily is relaxing on the living room rug, reading the latest edition of the *School Echoes*, a very worthwhile monthly publication taking in the Amish private schools in our community.

Brian is also reading. The local paper is his focal point. I'm guessing the sports pages are pretty well read word-for-word. He knows all sorts of sports facts—names, dates, you name it and he knows it. Sometimes he tells me things about a certain player or team. I listen but promptly forget because I have no more interest in such things. I don't mind listening to him though, as long as he still thinks I'm the most important person to talk too.

Colleen went to a friend's house for a girls' night out. They had plans to drive from there to Goshen for supper and some shopping.

Wayne went to the men's hymn practice.

Our five youngest think we live the most mundane, boring lives of all. We don't even compare to *anyone* else. The girls claim they never have anything exciting to tell their peers at school. Huh uh...never. Ernest's whole family went to the zoo. Harley's family all went to Chicago, and so go the stories. Yes, dears, maybe someday we can do that too.

When I point out our blessings, the children sigh. Emily might stomp her feet and declare, "I know, Mom, but so and so and so..." Oh, to teach my children true contentment in a materialized world. It *is* a blessing when our lives are normal and routine, even though boring. In fact, I can easily say I have never been bored, but my children sometimes think they are.

We never know when our lives could so drastically change; therefore, I am so thankful for each ordinary day. I firmly believe the more social events we plan, the more we have going, the bolder our children become. It's great to be satisfied at home.

We hear so many sad stories these days. Turmoil is all across the land. As the Christian churches are, so is the government. But let us dwell on the goodness around us. We are commanded to be joyful! For starters, we can find so much joy in our church services where we still hear the gospel. The flat out, full and simple gospel. Salvation. The plan. We are blessed with many sincere men who fervently seek and then share the message with us. I also find joy in the fellowship meal we all share.

I find joy in the ice-cream socials our neighborhood has during the summer months. Our comradeship is something to be thankful for. If I need to borrow something, I feel comfortable to go to any of my neighbors and ask. When we harvest, who helps? Our neighbors. We are supported by neighbors from birth, baptism, wedding, sickness, accidents, death—it makes no difference what the occasion. We are supported in love.

Many kind deeds are performed daily, quietly, joyously. Friendly smiles. Waves shared as we travel on the roads. These are things to rejoice in. Let's practice to dwell in these things instead of the gloom-iness we hear about.

Now, back to the scenes around me. Jolisa is taking a bath, loudly humming a medley of tunes. She can so easily entertain herself. In fact she loves to spend time by herself. The last two evenings, after school snacks and the chores she had to do, we all of a sudden realized we could not find her. We searched and called. We then thought she was back in the field with her daddy, but Karah had just come from back there and said she wasn't. We had called upstairs but not looked, so Colleen went upstairs and found her asleep on her bed. The second evening it didn't take us so long to find her. I guess her schoolwork wears her out. Emily and Jesse have a "homeless" shelter set up with blankets arranged over chairs, with the *only* possessions they own in their house. Lately we had a discussion on homeless people, so the subject is fresh in their minds.

Ten minutes to bedtime for the schoolgirls, so one by one they are taking their baths.

After supper and doing the dishes I went on my two-mile walk. My family thought I was pretty daft, as it was raining hard, but I needed to get out of the house to clear my mind. While walking along, a mini-van pulled up alongside me. I was surprised to see a former neighbor from my childhood days. We visited as fast as we could while I walked, making my walk in the rain doubly worthwhile. I came back to the house refreshed.

The dogs...yes, we still have the dogs. I don't plan on getting rid of Jacob, but Mandy, oh, I don't know. She's not so bad, and yet are we actually going to keep her? Jesse says we are; she's his friend. Brian says we aren't; she's in his way. I know one thing—she is ugly...so ugly, in fact, she's almost cute. I wish somebody would come get her, giving her a good home where she is wanted 100 percent. She loves playing with the children, giving them hugs in the morning or when we come home. Yet she can get pretty feisty when a stranger comes calling. She has her property marked and shows her loyalty and devotion to us. She loves to be bathed, but for me, I'm now enjoying the fact that my children are all able to bathe themselves. Spending time to bathe a dog? Are you kidding? Plus, she is an outside dog if she's living here, so she would look best bathed every day. I don't think so.

Jacob, on the other hand, is a big black, calm Lab. He too gives out hugs and sloppy kisses. He clearly adores all who live here. He reminds me a lot of Sam. We are definitely hooked on Labs. Today he helped Brian, Jesse, and me get a stray heifer to the place she was supposed to be. That made Jesse's day. He's pretty attached to his dogs.

As the children say, we are pretty boring. This time of the year, farmwork consists of hauling manure, feeding the 90 heifers, taking care of a dozen horses, and dealing with the two dogs. Then we haul manure, feed the heifers, the horses, and the dogs, scrape the barns, and haul more manure. A blessing...a blessing indeed.

◇◇◇◇◇

My heart is overflowing with feelings equaling goodwill and love for the people I was privileged to be involved with this past week. I'm seriously working on training my mind to think on the good in my life. The bad thoughts often threaten to overwhelm me, but I pray for guidance, for the good to take control, and to be truly happy.

Sunday forenoon, the beginning of a very busy week, we spent resting and reading at home. We enjoyed a brunch of grilled sausage patties (from the freezer), tomato gravy (fruit from the basement), and also fried potatoes (also summer bounty stored in the basement). In the afternoon we went to meet little Evan Matthew, the newest member of Wayne's niece JoEllen's family.

Monday was a beautiful wash day. Colleen wasn't working at the bakery that day, so she had the honor of filling the wash lines. In the evening was our monthly neighborhood gathering. I love these evenings except for the temptation of overindulging on the many delicious baked foods. I try to keep in mind Jesus' thoughts on taking care of our God-given temples. Do I need this or do I want this?

Tuesday I enjoyed cleaning the house a bit and preparing food for a surprise birthday party for Colleen. She is 17 already. A story all her own! She worked at the bakery that day, so once she got home she pampered herself with a nap. That gave me the opportunity to continue on with preparations and she stayed clueless. We'd invited Wayne's married nieces and nephews, and those with the youth. There were more than 40 people here! Colleen was surprised, and we immensely enjoyed our evening.

Wednesday Colleen was home to do laundry again. I canned applesauce and did various odd jobs that go with my occupation. We spent a deliciously lazy evening at home in the living room.

Thursday I canned apple-pie filling. Brian helped me out with that. I made apple crisp to take along to a friend's birthday surprise in the evening.

Friday morning I got to do the laundry, and then we cleaned house again. "We" being Brain and me. We had another birthday surprise planned for Colleen. We'd invited her friend Julie, Julie's boyfriend, Julie's parents and siblings, and another family of friends. I think Colleen had a good birthday.

Believe me when I say we hardly ever have more social plans then three or four evenings in a month. The children thought we were having a great time with plans four times in one week. They did pretty well with getting up in decent time for school in the morning, but they didn't have to do all the laundry, shopping, and other prepping our schedule created.

Friday evening after the company left, Wayne stretched out on the living room rug to relax while I finished cleaning up the house. He must have dozed off into a very deep slumber, as I told him a buggy drove in and he didn't respond. I got more aggressive. In an urgent voice I told him a buggy drove in and a guy was coming to the door. Wayne jumped up and came flying to the kitchen all wide-eyed and asking, "What is going on?" It was a neighbor asking to borrow a piece of equipment the next day. The guy left and Wayne told me he thought

I had said the heifers were out and there was one up here by the door. It was high time to get him to bed.

Saturday morning we got up early again, as we wanted to be on the road by 7:00. Wayne's brother, on the home place, wanted help with replacing some roofs, so they had a workday for Wayne's siblings. We ladies went along and helped Wayne's mom do some cleaning for church. We all enjoyed our day and wondered why we don't do things like that more often.

After lunch, Emily and I borrowed two of their bikes and biked to town for a few groceries. We fit our purchases in our bike baskets. I left the store feeling highly frustrated at having spent $60. I most certainly didn't get anything gourmet.

With field work at a standstill, Brian has more time on his hands than ever before. I can't handle someone just lying around during the day, so he's learning some new trades. He's discovered the joys of washing dishes, sweeping and mopping the floors, helping with the laundry, and doing some simple meal preparations—not to mention going to town with me to take care of the horse. I seem to be getting lazier by the day. He is so used to helping with the farmwork that he had thought of being incapable or it being only halfway necessary to be doing housework. But, hey, he won't ever be sorry to have learned. He doesn't know it yet, but I have great plans for him once I start washing off the walls and ceilings for church.

This week I have some much-needed sewing projects to do. As far as I know, I'll be home every day, and we only have plans for one evening, so I plan to accomplish a lot. I can dream big, but I will take one day at a time. Karah and Emily still need thick winter coats, plus dresses. I have fabric for a dress for myself, but I'd much rather sew for the others.

I also have some craft painting projects going, working on those to the wee hours of the morning. Takes a lot of coffee to keep me going. These hours will only be for a season though.

We will host church services on Christmas Day. It's also our turn to host Wayne's family Christmas gathering, planned for the thirtieth.

Christmas is a special time, a time of rejoicing in the Lord. It's a wonderful time to praise God, be glad in him, continue on in prayer, and remember God's promises to those who truly love him. Be thankful in all things. Acknowledge where we come from, and count our many blessings.

We've still got the dogs! This morning while it was still dark, I was bent over the generator plugging in the cord to do the laundry when something touched me! I whirled around ready to do battle, and there stands Jacob as innocent as can be. He got my blood pressure up in a hurry.

Year 5

Winter

Wayne wonders how I ever survived the time I helped chore four hours a day, plus had my hands full with our little children. I wonder too. During that time I invited company over for supper a lot more than I do now, and my memory (is it playing tricks on me?) tells me I wasn't any more harried than I am now.

Whose fault is it? My own. I have no one else to blame except me. Several things play a factor, I suppose. Number one, it seems being a mother becomes much more challenging as the children grow. We get older. Even though I feel better than I did when the children were small, I probably do move slower. There are so many decisions to make each day, and then the greatest struggle for me is sticking to the decisions I make. I think it's children's nature to push their mom for all she's worth. Another challenge is to keep them busy yet happy.

The three youngest girls haven't learned to associate work and happiness in the same category yet. Being penned up in this house during the winter just adds to their misery. Sure, they do go outside, but to them it seems the inside work is endless and miserable. I tell them that all who wish to participate in our family must help pull the load. We do not tolerate slackers. They forget about the free time they have.

Four or five nights a week the children and I go over to Ida's basement to walk, rollerblade, Ripstik, play dodgeball, or some sort of ball game for heart-thumping exercise. We spend at least 30 minutes down there. Long enough to get red-faced and sweaty, be ready to head back to our house, want to shower and go to bed. I strongly believe in being physically active, plus I find this a very enjoyable time with my children. Another factor of all these crazy schedules is the rebirth of my acrylic painting. For 11 years I put that hobby on the back shelf. Every once in a while I would paint something for a gift or some greeting cards, but nothing major. Well, now I am painting again. My first big event for painting was for a Christmas crafters sale at a big event center in November. I was pleased with the reception of my products, plus I really enjoyed working with the public. I enjoyed the two days at the sale so much I actually felt guilty.

The next week I hurriedly sewed some dresses for Jolisa, and one for myself, amongst other motherly duties. I also had a canister set to paint for someone, plus a sizeable paint order to have done to take along to Ohio that weekend. Wayne and I were planning on going to a book-signing for my cookbook in Berlin. Is this busyness worth it? I did get done with Wayne and the children's help. They fully support me. Without their support I wouldn't even attempt this business.

Brian perfected his domestic skills by helping me be ready when the driver came on Friday morning. He can handle the broom pretty well. He conned Jesse into doing the breakfast dishes though. Today when I retrieved a pot from the cupboard to cook pancake syrup, I wondered what had been severely burned in it...as there was plenty of evidence left in the pot. The girls informed me it was from Brian's cooking one of the days I was gone. He'd heated rice. I wonder how it tasted. I'm convinced it had extra flavor.

◇◇◇◇◇

Wayne and I arrived in Holmes County, Ohio, on Friday afternoon. We immensely enjoyed our tour of Carlisle Printing. We then enjoyed supper and fellowship on the Michael Miller farm with friends. We joined our friends Daniel, Mae, and their son Tristan in their surrey to journey to their house for the night. We got a true taste of their hills when their horse Cody couldn't keep his footing trying to pull us up one of those hills. My surrey door was open for a quick escape. It wasn't necessary. Daniel and Tristan soon had everything under control.

I had commissioned my sister Ida to bake some cream pies for us to take along, as that seemed to be a new recipe for our Buckeye friends. I also baked some, although I am not a pro like Ida is. These proved to be a hit and a conversation favorite when ladies showed interest in my cookbooks at the book signing. One lady came back to us showing that she'd bought cream to bake this pie. Ohio might be famous for Trail bologna and Swiss cheese, but Indiana (at least my family) has baked cream pies!

We arrived home safe and sound at 8:15, tired and ready to see the children again. They had done a super job of keeping the home fires burning. Jesse had been sick with a fever and stomachache, but they had done well in taking care of him. They were all ready for bed when we got home, but they listened to our stories before retiring.

Wayne says they want to haul all the manure this week. Brian is disassembling a windbreak behind the barn that was damaged by high winds. There is always something to be done outside. If nothing else, Brian can clean up after the dogs. They are still here, they still make messes, they still work on my nerves, I am still overruled.

Colleen and I began cleaning for church. We have now cleaned out most of the kitchen cupboards. That proves to be a time-consuming job—to wash all the canisters and organize everything. The Tupperware behind those doors can be horrific, as is the small-container lid drawer. Now everything looks and feels so nice. I gave the girls a lesson on putting the dishes away and always in the same spot. I want to clean out several more cupboards—a good day or two's worth—and then start with walls, furniture, and such. I am anxious to begin because it is so necessary.

◇◇◇◇◇

I've been trying new soup recipes this winter. I love soup. My children say, "Soup again?" followed by moaning and groaning. But, hey, soup goes with our lifestyle—simple, warm, and filling.

◇◇◇◇◇

Jolisa is jump-roping here in the kitchen, just a flyin'. In the meantime, the girls are taking turns setting the table. Karah put on the plates and glasses. Jolisa will fill the glasses with water. Emily is putting on the silverware. They make sure no one does more or less than the other. I basically grew up alone, but my girls are pros at sibling rivalry. Fairness must be practiced to a T, no matter that they are not the exact same age. Motherhood is not for sissies.

Now they are playing horse. Jesse is driving Emily, and Jolisa is driving Karah. Brian is teasing them, thinking they are too old to be playing horsey. They are, but such is life in the middle of winter with the children's pent-up energy. Most of them are barefooted because part of the kitchen floor is so slippery. My mistake. We bought new shoes for the three schoolgirls, and Wayne told me to spray them with silicone as an added protective cover. I did and I thought I was okay with spraying them on a carpet, but it wasn't okay. The spray floated all over, making it outright dangerous to walk sock-footed in the kitchen. We're liable to break some bones. The children admitted they are glad it was mama because they surely would have been reprimanded.

Today Colleen did the laundry and some cleaning up. After breakfast, sweeping and mopping the floor, and getting the girls to school, I got some mail ready to send. The rest of the forenoon I spent on a writing project. I fixed some leftovers and a salad for lunch, and then I wrote all afternoon again. That's all I got accomplished. It kind of gave me the blues.

For supper we're having more leftover "chicken and Tater Tot" casserole, green beans, and applesauce. Popcorn will be good once we settle in the living room. I have to walk at least 20 minutes yet before I can relax. I have pent-up energy that needs to be calmed. It was a drab, dreary day, making me long for spring.

Today Brian cleaned both the horse and heifer barns, worked with his yearling colt, and got the horses out of a field they weren't supposed to be in twice. He also raked part of the yard for me. After a heavy snowfall, so many small twigs were on the ground looking messy. The snow all melted, making it possible for him to rake.

Karah, Emily, and Jolisa fixed their lunches and swept the house before they went to school. I had some proofreading and other paperwork to do. After the girls left for school, Brian, Jesse, and I went across the driveway to Ida's house to clean her basement. We scrubbed the walls and floor, getting it ready to host church services and various gatherings. Brian's long legs and arms came in handy to clean the pipes that I couldn't reach. He would've rather been outside, but he gave up and helped me until we were done. Jesse played with a SuperBall he found down there. Little guy has to entertain himself these days. He is six years old already. He discovered he can draw. His imagination and pencil work well together. Anyway, it was high time for lunch by the time we got back to our house.

This afternoon I worked on painting pictures on a big, white, wooden toy box that someone ordered. Time got away from me as I was thoroughly enjoying myself. It has a little girl's name in balloon letters, flowers, a puppy, a ladybug, a dragonfly, a turtle, a butterfly, and some froggies. I had not undertaken a project like this in a long time, and it was fun.

After supper, Wayne and I walked the three-fourths mile to school for the monthly meeting with the teachers. We were too early, so we continued to walk a while longer, turned back, and then stood outside talking until it was time to go in. I thoroughly enjoyed our date! Walking home together under the starry sky was relaxing to the max. We needed that time together.

The house was quiet when we came home. The children had showered and were in bed. The three schoolgirls, of course, came downstairs wanting to know what their teachers had to say about them. I asked them if they were guilty about something, and they didn't think they were. No, they had nothing to worry about.

◇◇◇◇◇

After doing the mid-week laundry, sweeping the house, and washing the dishes, Colleen, Jesse, and I went across the driveway to Ida's house again to continue with the cleaning. My stepmom, Alice, also helped us, which I really appreciated. We cleaned the two bedrooms, extra bath, and sewing room. It feels good and clean.

After lunch break, I washed the curtains and doilies. It was a beautiful, sunny day for doing laundry. Colleen took care of our dry laundry. Once the girls were home from school, they swept the house. Where does all the dirt come from?

After our supper of cheesy potato soup, garlic dill pickles, and red beets, Emily, Jolisa, and Jesse did a great job of doing the dishes. They completely cleared the counters, wiped the stove front, and swept the crumbs from under the table. I praised them for the job well done.

◇◇◇◇◇

Emily stayed home from school today as she started with a bad cold. Karah also has it, but hopefully the bug will stop there. The children just now informed me that the dog chewed up the new four-way plugin I keep in the mudroom.

Mandy is in serious trouble. She about wrapped up her death sentence. She is so protective of us—too protective—as she has gotten hold of too many socks and shoes of people coming to the door. I can't handle that. Jacob is very protective of us too. His size is very intimidating to people, but he is a gentle giant. The dogs slept on bunk beds in the mudroom, pushing the boots off the shelves. One slept on the bottom shelf; the other one the second shelf. Come morning, we had to organize the boots on the shelves again. That era must come to a close. I will resume ownership of the mudroom. We'll put a box or an old blanket out there for Jacob.

The clock shows 4:40 AM. My cup of Starbucks Colombian coffee is depleted already. Hopefully it will do its job well and give me the boost I need. I need a mentality kick too! My devotions also contributed to a fresh start to the day. I am reading the interesting stories of Abraham. How very different our lives are and yet so similar. We are failing humans in need of a Savior.

The house is quiet except for the ticking of the clock and the warm hum of the gas lamp above me. Wayne left for work 10 minutes ago, and the six children are still in bed. I savor this moment. Too bad my coffee is all gone, and I'm too lazy to go make another cup.

I am surely enjoying these slower months. Slow months? That's how I tend to label the months between Christmas and spring. They haven't been exactly slow for me, but I make the bed I lie in. I think I have hobbyitis. I just pieced two quilts for my sister Leanna's quilt shop. Next week I need to work on paint orders and also sew for the family. My family is not neglected. Sometimes they are sorely underprivileged though...just ask them. I believe they are very normal children. The schoolgirls' line is that they always have to wear the same school dresses. *Gasp!* Did you hear that? Every week, week after week. Always the same ones. I do laundry three times a week, and I remind them they always have a clean dress to wear. I do not think it necessary to have more than four school dresses. They have more dresses to wear if we have plans in the evening, plus their Sunday and everyday dresses. No, they are not underprivileged at all. We are blessed—blessed indeed.

◇◇◇◇◇

I am bummed out at packing lunches. There are five that need to be filled. Wayne still wants a sandwich for the convenience of not having to wait in line to use the microwave. Colleen wants leftovers from supper, rice, or a salad. I'd be so sick and tired of eating those things, but I guess I often eat the same simple things for my lunch too. The schoolgirls' tastes vary so much. Right now Jolisa's into toasted cheese sandwiches. Yesterday morning she almost cried when I asked her what she's having for lunch. The girls fix their own lunches, but I knew if she wanted a toasted cheese, I'd have to make it for her. She said she wanted one, but the other girls at school tease her that that's the only thing she eats. I convinced her that it doesn't matter, and soon she was her happy self again. They all eat peaches almost every day. Canned or frozen, frozen or canned, it doesn't vary too much. Sometimes they'll take yogurt. Swiss Roll Cake is a favorite among most of them. Brian eats that like it's going out of style. He eats anything like crazy, and it's no wonder with the way he keeps growing. He towers over me.

Brian is prepping his colt, Lancer, to sell at the Topeka horse sale. Clipping, exercising, leading, and feeding some oily supplement of some kind. He was concerned Lancer wouldn't eat his feed with the new top dressing, so at 8:00 last night he went outside to check. He was happy to report that the young horse had eaten it all. He spends a lot of time with Lancer, and I hope he does well at the sale.

I asked Brian if I should go with him to the sale because Wayne would be working. He said sure! You know I am not a horse-sale person, but I'm guessing Jesse and I will go. I actually enjoy the horse sale— watching the horses, the wildly stepping men and boys that lead the horses, and the interesting ramble of the auctioneers. It's the crowd that keeps me home in my comfort zone.

Jesse looks forward to the horse sale. He is one bored six-year-old. One winter morning, I was hanging up laundry over our coal stove in the kitchen when he came to me asking what he could do. I sighed. Then he said, "I know, Mom. Here we go again!" We got him more preschool workbooks to work in, a wooden toy set, and a 1/16-scale backhoe for his Christmas and birthday presents thinking that would give him something different to do. His Aunt Ida gave him a skid loader that makes sounds—something that he's been wishing for, for a long time already. Now, I have to remind him to play with it. Yesterday Wayne made a pallet for the skid loader, so Jesse was hauling blocks around last night. Hopefully that will last a while. He's more into writing and drawing, and he does spend a lot of time with pencil and paper. He won't go to school yet next term, but maybe I will need to homeschool him to keep him occupied.

My sister Ida gave the girls a Sizzix for Christmas. It's a wonderful little hand-cranked machine that gives homemade cards unique character. It's given the girls hours of fun already. The girls have a table set up on the porch, and every evening after the supper dishes are done they are making pretty cards. I think they need to open a store.

This warm winter weather we've been having has been wonderful for me. So far I've not had to deal with cabin fever nearly as much as usual, probably because of the beautiful, sunny, laundry-drying days we've had.

For Wayne and Brian, it's been more frustrating because of the mud. Everything is so dirty outside. Hauling manure is so frustrating because the fields are way too soft to drive on. Plus they can't pile the manure because it isn't frozen.

One Monday that Brian could haul manure also happened to be a beautiful wash day. I didn't realize how bad the manure smell was outside because I was just in the house after I was done hanging the laundry outside. That evening while wiping my face on a towel after a shower, I realized how bad the smell must have been. The next day Wayne said he could smell it on his clothes all day and was very conscious of it. I could have cried. Our Sunday clothes marinated in manure! The towels smelled the worst though, especially after they were wet. Oh well, could've been something worse.

Year 5

Spring

Hallelujah! It's a beautiful 70-degree spring day! The birds are singing; a gentle breeze is blowing. The children are outside playing. That's reason enough to celebrate. Even though we had a mild winter, spring was joyfully anticipated.

This afternoon Wayne, Colleen, and I butchered a small pig. Our shop stays nice and cool—cool enough to cool down the meat yet it was pleasantly warm to work outside. The meat is ready for the freezer. That's a good feeling. Another thing to rejoice about is the fact that the meat grinder and all the tubs and big bowls used to butcher are washed sparkling clean, and put away.

One really sore spot in my day is the fact that I cut my middle finger on my left hand pretty badly. I absolutely despise wearing Band-Aids. They gross me out. There was no way I could avoid using one with this cut though because I bled severely. Now I've got this chunky finger that somewhat handicaps me. I know it's minor, like a hobble or call it a speed bump, which is definitely true. One good thing though is I can't wash dishes. Oh groan, now I thought of the laundry in the morning. How am I going to do that? Colleen has to work at the bakery, and the three little girls are in school. Brian informs me he is busy all day. I think Karah will have to get up early so she can help me before she goes to school.

◇◇◇◇◇

This afternoon after school, two neighbor children, Jeremy and Kayla, came to play. Jeremy brought his pony, Princess, and the children all took turns riding her. Once Jeremy was back on her, she decided that was enough and bucked Jeremy to a crash landing on the driveway. Away ran Princess! She ran to momentary freedom in our pasture. Our big mare Jenny was surprised at such a visitor and did not welcome Princess at all.

Brian finally caught her after Wayne and Karah got their exercise. Brian decided to ride her too. His long legs touched the ground on either side. After riding about 50 feet at a cute little gait, Brian's legs tangled with Princess's front legs. Immediately Brian was on the ground and Princess was running to freedom again. You had to be there! It was hilarious. I got my daily dose of a belly laugh right there, with chuckles following every once in a while.

◇◇◇◇◇

After our supper of fresh barbeque ribs, a vegetable medley, noodles, and plenty of conversation, the dishes were quickly washed by Emily and dried and put away by Karah. Colleen, Jolisa, and I did other odd jobs of clearing the table, sweeping the floor, and cleaning the stove top.

Brian went to a neighbor boy's birthday party. Colleen went for a walk. Jolisa and Karah helped me take the fresh meat to the freezer. Then I went on my walk. It was a beautiful, calm evening. As I walked along, I heard the birds singing their praises to our Lord. I saw many well-kept homesteads full of fresh vigor for the coming summer.

My favorite stretch of walking is past a lush, dark-green pasture dotted with a beautiful, well-kept herd of Jersey cows. They were leaving the feed bunk and heading for the pasture. Oftentimes some of the cows come to the fence to check me out, their curiosity getting the best of them. They contentedly chew their cuds.

On one farm, the chickens were scratching the ground one last time before heading to their nests to roost for the night. All was quiet, peaceful. My gaze swept across the countryside as I continued north and crested a knob. I saw a lot more homesteads. I didn't see pride in these homes, just good stewardship honoring our heavenly Father. I turned around and head back home.

Except for my throbbing finger, it has been a very good day. Coming home, I see the girls riding their bikes, flying around the circle drive. Jesse is pulling a wagon with Jacob getting a ride! Jacob loves to get a ride. He's big enough; he should be the one pulling the wagon.

At bedtime Brian is not at home yet, so Jesse is dizzying around here, not wanting to go to bed without his big brother. He is playing with three bean bag chairs. Sometimes all I see are his feet flying through the air, flipping under the bags. Then he stacks them on top of each other and tries to climb to the top. Doesn't work. Most of the time he is talking nonstop. Mom is mentioned many times. He's got his nightshirt and trunks on, plus a bandana tied around his neck because he's got a cold. It smells like he's got half a bottle of Vick's VapoRub ointment smeared on him. He's got socks on his feet that he also slathered with Vick's in hopes he can sleep without coughing all night.

Colleen is not working at the bakery today, so I will greedily take advantage of having her at home. We need to do the laundry and the weekly ironing, amongst other things. I should spray some unsightly weeds. Colleen needs to thoroughly clean the upstairs, as it is our turn to host my family's monthly family night this coming Monday.

Wayne hopes to be home from work by 10:00 or soon after, and then we want to go to Shipshewana to get some groceries, go to the bank, and stop at the hardware store. Jesse gets to go along, so he is out of the house so Colleen can clean faster.

Brian is working for a local jack-of-all-trades kind of guy. They clean up ditch banks, old train beds, split wood—whatever anyone wants done. Brian hasn't enjoyed all the stone picking he's had to do in long, dusty fields. Colleen shows him no mercy, telling him to be quiet and that the work will help make him a man. This job is good for him, plus if we have field work or something, he can stay home to do that.

The schoolgirls learned new songs for their "last day of school" program. I love to hear the three of them singing together. Their voices are so different and blend beautifully. I have always loved to sing, and as a girl growing up often longed for siblings my age to sing with. Now I feel fortunate to sing with the girls. Wayne and the boys can sing too if I can persuade them to join us. The shower is Wayne's singing stage, but we don't all fit in the bathroom to join in the melody. It's humbling to me that we are commanded to sing unto the Lord.

This spring the weather has been unlike any I remember ever having experienced in my life. It was wonderful except for the hard frosts we had in mid-April when the hayfields were lush and green. Even with the strawberries covered with old sheets and plastic, I still picked off some blackened flowers. We had strawberries blooming in April and asparagus to eat in March. That's a month earlier than normal.

Brian and I biked to Shipshewana on a beautiful day in April. We were embarrassingly warm when we got there. Unreal for April.

We had a taste of hospital life with Wayne's mom being in the LaGrange hospital for nine days. While preparing to do laundry one Monday morning, she suddenly experienced excruciating pain and vomiting. It was discovered her hernia had ruptured. Surgery was done around 4:00 in the afternoon, and by that time gangrene had already started. She was a very sick lady. She has a long recovery ahead but is doing well considering the circumstances.

While she was at the hospital, Wayne and I biked the 12.5 miles to see her on a Saturday night. On the way we stopped at Emma Café, an old-fashioned, small-town soda shop. We ate butter pecan ice-cream cones and sipped some Pepsi before heading on east. We needed some calories to burn. It was fun. It took us an hour biking time. We stayed the night with Wayne's mom, and then we biked home in the morning. It took us an hour and a half going home because we faced a strong wind.

We had company for Sunday dinner, but the other ladies brought most of the meal. The girls had the house ready and the table set.

By evening we were tired! On Monday, Wayne said he thought he slept on the basement floor last night because he slept so deeply. It was all worthwhile though, and I would do it again.

While at the hospital we met other hurting families, plus experienced some rejoicing from new additions to their families. I thought, *Once we get home we want to continue praying for people in the hospital, known and unknown.* So soon I am caught up in my daily grind and forget about the hospital life. Shame.

◇◇◇◇◇

"If God brings you to it, he will bring you through it." When our children were small, plus with three or four hours in the barn each day, women would often tell me, "This too shall pass." Sometimes those words angered me, and I would retort, "If I shall last!" I understood, knowing their words were meant to bring comfort and encouragement, but the failing human I am, I didn't always accept them for what they were intended.

One of the nicest things anyone ever did for me during those times was a neighbor lady who left her work lying and came to help me several days doing whatever needed doing. Her companionship and love were sweeter than honey to my soul. Doing good deeds like that for other people does not come naturally for me. I am ashamed to admit it. As the Lord continues to shape and mold me, I pray to do better. To let the Lord work through me. I absolutely love my neighbors and church people. Why then do I not let them know? What is love if it doesn't have action?

⬦⬦⬦⬦⬦

It is still early morning, but I now hear Brian's alarm going off. Soon the house will be buzzing with activity. They will all want breakfast. It takes lots of pancakes or French toast for Brian. Colleen, Karah, and I want a breakfast sandwich consisting of one-half whole wheat English muffin and egg. Emily can hardly swallow breakfast. Jolisa loves toast with homemade strawberry jam. Jesse is unpredictable, wanting oatmeal, toast and egg, or cereal. Hard telling which one. Such is life on our farm.

⬦⬦⬦⬦⬦

A brand-new week! I work at rousing Karah and Emily on this beautiful Monday morning. I tell them the washing machine is loaded already, although I don't know if telling them is a good idea. It might slow their steps further. I've let them sleep until eight o'clock, but now it is time to shift gears and move forward. I've filled the washing machine, started the generator, and put in the Sunday whites to soak a while. Jesse's white shirt was terribly dirty.

Summer vacation started with a few bumps and bruises, but we are pretty well adjusted and enjoying the girls at home. It goes best when everybody is busy and knows which direction they're headed. One particular Monday all four girls were in the kitchen trying to help each other make lunch. What a ruckus! I reminded Colleen why it's a good idea that she has a job this summer. She was glad she could go to work the rest of the week. She was used to having the kitchen to herself this winter and almost felt violated.

Karah is learning to cook in mini strides. I think I will have her bake something today after they are done with the laundry. She is still unsure of herself when cooking or baking, so I will stay close by. Karah and Emily have been on laundry duty since school was out. I'm quickly getting used to that. Jolisa does the dishes and sweeps the floors while the others do the laundry. They then all have to help each other bring in, fold, and put away the laundry. They, of course, get tired of it, but I think it is a wonderful opportunity to teach them to be faithful in many ways. Faithful in well doing, faithful in obeying their parents, faithful in participating in keeping the household running smoothly, along with being faithful in unity and putting joy into a repetitious job.

◇◇◇◇◇

With the stress of corn planting now on the side, Wayne is slightly undecided what he wants to do this afternoon when he comes home from work. He wants to either cut some hay or go help one of the neighbors with their hay. By the end of the week I'm sure he'll have done both.

We've enjoyed watching our two draft horse colts playing in the small field west of the house. The babies seem healthy and were able to nurse on their own from the start. That was a huge relief for me.

◇◇◇◇◇

Emily, now 10 years old, planted the sweet corn in the garden. Her older siblings teased her about her crooked rows, but they actually weren't. The girls like to help with the garden planting, except for the potato planting, which can be backbreaking. They do make a lot of steps for me; it takes a strong mind to stay calm and organized.

◇◇◇◇◇

Wayne bought us a new buggy horse at the sale this spring. Getting used to a new horse can be a challenge. We need to learn to know each other. This steed looked a tad ugly, but Wayne thought with some wormer and lots of good feed he'd perk right up. He's only a four-year-old, so hopefully we can keep him a while—if he turns out okay.

Brian brushed him up, Wayne gave him the wormer, and I gave

him his name: Max. We had him for a week-and-a-half when I drove him to my friend's house for the day. It was the farthest we had driven him and the first time to take him on US 20. It was just me and Jesse, and Jesse refused to ride with me in the front.

Max shied about some *Haflingers** in a pasture and some signs at the bridge, but he never once flinched about the trucks that roared past us on the highway. He got us safely there and home again.

Year 5

Summer

We love this summer weather, but we're praying for rain. Our crops are suffering because of the lack of moisture. Wayne tells me not to make a fuss; God is in control.

◇◇◇◇◇

Cleaning out the cupboards, sewing on a dress, and working on a paint order are on the agenda for today. On my morning walk, I noticed several things that need to be watered, so the girls can do that and harvest some things from the garden. They also need to clean the north end of the buggy shed. They have their stamping supplies set up out there, and it's in dire need of organizing. They've spent many happy hours there. Sometimes a neighbor girl named Sharon joins them, much to their delight.

◇◇◇◇◇

With Wayne and Brian both working off the farm long hours this spring, it created a challenge to take care of the crops. Brian was at home two days in a row so he could spray the cornfields. One such morning he was spraying, I was picking strawberries, and Karah and Emily were doing laundry. All of a sudden our peace was shattered with the sound of a team of horses come galloping up the lane!

From the sound I knew they'd hit the cement between the barns at full blast! I couldn't see them because of buildings, but I moved quickly, praying instantly and constantly. I was afraid! Where was Brian? Were the girls out of the way? How would I stop those huge horses? Then CRASH! And all was quiet. With the force of the crash I knew if Brian had still been on the cart, he would have flown off now. As I rounded the house, I saw Brian coming up the lane, and he appeared to be okay. The horses and the *forecart** were in the barn, but the sprayer was stuck outside the barn.

Whew! Relief! Brian was okay, and with some minor repairs on the sprayer and the barn door, all would be well.

Brian and my dad got the horses unhitched, hitched to another cart, and then they went several miles to a shop with *haybines*.* Brian said the horses needed work! I went back to the strawberry patch still weak from the excitement and filled with thankfulness that no one had been hurt.

These horses are normally not spooky like that, but when Brian left the forecart to raise the booms of the sprayer, they took off. We think they could only see the booms from the corners of their eyes and were startled, plus being well fed and full of pep they decided to head home.

June 2 was picked out for the day a group of us friends wanted to go to Fort Wayne to garage sales. I was excited because it had been 12 years since I had last gone. Most of the other women said their men were going along too. I tried to convince mine to go along. I figured the chances were slim to none because he figures that's not something he would enjoy. When I mentioned it to him, trying to convince him to go along, he threw me off, giving me no satisfaction. Going to garage sales? Whatever!

Well, that morning I got up at 4:45 and got ready. The driver was to start picking up at 5:00. At 5:00, Wayne rolls over in bed and says, "What shall I do?"

I said, "What do you mean, 'What shall you do'?" He perfectly well knew what he wanted to work that day. We repeated that several times when I discovered he was actually thinking about going along! I was astonished to say the least.

He went and we had a blast! The fun time we spent with friends was just as fun, or more so, than the garage sales. Now I want to go again. The bug bit me. But, alas, now I need to clean for church, garden, sew, and paint. Yes, life goes on without me going garage-saling again this week.

◇◇◇◇◇

I didn't buy peaches to can this year because they were pretty well golden. Sixty dollars a bushel for Baby Gold peaches, which is what I normally can. Figuring I get 25 quarts per bushel, that's $2.40 a quart. By the time I add the sugar and can lids, I'd be pushing $3 a quart. We like the Aldi brand peaches, so that is what we will be eating this year. I did freeze Red Haven and Carolina peaches in small containers for lunches. Those weren't quite so expensive. We like to make slush with frozen peaches, strawberries, and 7UP, but that will need to be limited this year.

It's also the season of hobo pies and s'mores by the fire. It takes a lot of s'more supplies with growing children. Mom and Dad like them too. Our favorite is still the Ritz cracker, Hershey bar ones with roasted marshmallows oozing out the sides.

◇◇◇◇◇

I used Max to go to town, and he does okay...except he doesn't back up. That is a must in town—to back away from the hitching rail. Wayne must put in another bit to see if that will help. He's got one tough mouth. Max doesn't look like the same horse we bought. Feed and exercise have done him a lot of good.

We bought another horse named Daisy. I haven't driven her yet. They say she backs up fine, stands good to hitch and at corners, and goes a good clip. She's a sharp-looking little mare. We got rid of our old horse, Girl. She gave us years of service, but the older she got the ornerier she got. The children cheered when the truck came to get her because they had hated when we'd use her.

Brian says he will be home the next few days, so I'm putting him to work. The old, glazed-tile building needs cleaning out, except the area of the woodshed where the girls have their playhouse. There is plenty of trash to be burned and just general cleanup. He is one handy guy to have around.

The girls' playhouse has changed to a store right now. Sometimes I go to the pantry to get an item I want and can't find it. I'm pretty positive I still have some, so I search some more. Then it dawns on me, "Oh, it's probably out in the store!" Jolisa is exactly as I remember myself at her age. Having a store was a huge dream, and I had one on our old back porch for a long time. Making paper money, signs...well, anything having to do with a store and paper, was a blast. I wonder how many receipt books I filled out for my pretend customers. I saved all the paper too—anything, for that matter, until my drawers moaned and groaned and bulged under the weight. I wish I could ask my mom some questions now. I'm sure of the fact that she would agree Jolisa inherited my jumpy busyness. I have slowed down though. Oh my, yes I sure have.

"Be joyful in hope, patient in affliction, faithful in prayer" (Romans 12:12 NIV). God's promises are still that: God's promises. Even in these perilous times we live in. He did not promise us all joys and no sorrows, but he did promise to be with us every step of the way.

For these last several months, it seems God has shut off all water faucets from the heavens. No rain period. Every morning the sun comes up gorgeous; every night the sun goes down gorgeous. A long time ago they said if we don't get rain in the next few days the crops will surely fail. That was weeks ago and still no rain. Our corn has had less than half-an-inch of rain since the planting in May. You can only imagine what it looks like.

We do water the garden a bit, but does it justify the money spent on diesel to pump the water? I had thought the green beans looked decent because the plants were loaded with flowers. When I went out to pick the first picking, the bugs had eaten into many of the beans. As I picked, I threw away at least half of the beans. I promptly sprayed the plants and hope to harvest enough to can later. I'm guessing the insect's food supply is low too, and they were searching for new delectables. The yellow summer squash plants died on me too. We've only gotten enough of those for one meal, and then it wasn't enough for Wayne and me. We let the children eat them.

We had high hopes of feeding heifers again this winter with our own feed. We are again reminded of who is in control. We are just as children. We sometimes need to be reminded in a clear, loud voice and learn to be content as the Lord sees fit. I thank him for the reminder.

◇◇◇◇◇

The week of July Fourth my sister Freda and some of her family from Oklahoma visited here for a week. During that time we had two big family reunions here, so we had cleaned the shop good for those days. Now for church in two weeks we only need to give it a good going over. That was the week of 110 degrees. *Mercy!* We did survive. It took a lot of water. The evening we had the Rabers (my mom's family) here it took 25 gallons of water.

Since Freda was here she's gained another granddaughter named Edna Irene. That name is mighty precious and gave me a fresh dose of longing to see my mom, whose name was Edna.

◇◇◇◇◇

This morning Karah and Emily were again doing laundry. With cleaning for church, there is always laundry to do. It almost makes me sick though because it's so terribly dusty. Cleaning seems to be in vain. Even the laundry comes back in from the lines dusty.

Halfway into laundry, the girls convinced me to wash the upstairs bedding, doilies, and curtains. They'd much rather clean the whites (sashes) of the windows. I thought they didn't know what they were getting into. I'd much rather do the laundry then wash those whites. I took up their plea, and they did super.

This afternoon Karah ironed the doilies and some of the curtains while I washed the upstairs windows. The two girls put all the things back in place. They want to be stylish so they hardly have anything standing on their furniture, especially nothing childish. They were all excited because I finally took the time to paint some sayings and daisies on their walls. Now they sigh and say they still need to get rid of those girlie curtains. They really need something more mature. I should say so. After all, they are 11, 10, and 8. Mature indeed.

Yesterday I scrubbed and rewaxed the kitchen floor. After all the time and energy it took, it doesn't feel clean as it normally does. I discovered because of the open windows dust had settled on the wet wax and dried into the finished product. It appears clean but is a tad rough.

I've had to think of the people in Kansas who endured the "dirty '30s." We might not have dust storms, but we do have a lot of traffic on our dirt road, including semitrucks, school buses, cement trucks, dump trucks, and hordes of other traffic. They don't go slow just because I don't like the dust. No, they've got places to go to in a hurry. I guess I'm thankful for that too. All this traffic means the world is going on, and people have work and places to go. But must they go so fast?

For supper tonight I used a grill basket to grill chunks of button mushrooms, green and red peppers, onions, pineapple, and smoked sausages. We love kabobs, but it is easier to just toss it all into the grill basket. I tossed a salad of cucumbers, cauliflower, and lettuce. For dessert we had fresh peaches and blueberries. Pure summer!

Last week one evening I made homemade tortillas. We filled them with grilled chicken breast strips, onions, peppers, sour cream, and BBQ sauce. These were delicious. They were also very simple to make and were filled with whatever we had on hand.

I told Wayne that with the cabbage ripe in the garden I want to make egg rolls again. Several of the children groaned, but I want them to give egg rolls one more chance. I didn't like them the first time I ate them either.

With school starting before long, I will have some major withdrawal symptoms to deal with. Withdrawal from my girls. I'll be lost without their help. It'll just be Jesse and me. And Jacob, who cries outside the door if we ignore him for too long. I tease Wayne that he talks sweeter to the dog than he does to me.

Karah will be in the sixth grade this year, Emily in the fourth, and Jolisa in the third. Karah and Emily are growing like weeds, catching up with me. Jolisa is still quite a bit shorter than her sisters. She's curly haired, freckled, and always bouncy. She's gotten the brunt of washing dishes this summer. Jesse was to help her this forenoon, but finally she couldn't handle his dawdling so she sent him on his merry way.

I wanted to treat the girls to a day in town before school started, so this morning I did the laundry. By 8:00, Brian, Karah, Emily, Jolisa, Jesse, and I went to the Shipshewana Flea Market to get school shoes and some dishrags I really like. We also loaded up on socks. We didn't get much else. It all fit in one handbag, minus the shoes.

It was 12:00 by the time we were done at the flea market. We met my sister-in-law Nettie and her six daughters at East of Chicago Pizza for lunch. We had met them at the flea market, so we planned to meet for lunch. The children all thought it was a grand idea.

After a leisurely lunch we walked across the road to the fabric store.

I bought fabric for Sunday dresses for Karah, Emily, and Jolisa. I also needed fabric for a shirt for Wayne and school dresses for Emily and Jolisa. By that time I was so tired I could hardly think straight. When I got out to the buggy, Brian informed me with emphasis that we'd taken half an hour. Way too long, according to him. He was very patient with me all day though. In fact, all the children did super.

On the way to E&S, the bulk-food store, the road was extremely busy, so I dreaded the thought of crossing the road to enter the parking lot and then to get back on the road again. That is a hazard we face going to town with the horse and buggy. We survived but not without stress. Our horse was extremely tired of waiting by then. We had to wait a while on a break in traffic, and then he was a bit unruly.

We traveled on to Dollar General to stock up on toiletries and cereal, and then we headed home. It was past 3:00 by that time.

There was laundry and groceries to put away, floors to be swept, a cape and apron to finish for a wedding that Colleen wanted to go to that evening. Plus supper to make, and cucumbers to harvest, and...

Then a neighbor lady came to ask if we would babysit her small son from 4:00 to 9:30 tonight. That turned out to be a big, major blessing because it put pep into the girls' steps, motivating them to get their jobs done so they could play with Adrian.

I had to set the timer at five-minute intervals, two for work, and one for babysitting so all was done in perfect fairness. For three sisters born in three years and three months' time, perfect fairness is very important. Luckily this little Adrian loves their smothering attention.

Supper was kept extremely simple. Toasted cheese with tomato sandwiches and muskmelons from the garden. The girls finished cleaning up the kitchen and are now spraying off the walks and some of the buggy wheels. Wayne is working on the silage chopper head again. Seems that thing gets lots of attention. He's just making sure all is in perfect working condition for when harvest begins.

The girls also got their school supplies ready. I overheard them say that gathering their supplies does make them excited to begin another school year.

Tomorrow two of my sisters, two sisters-in-law, and my married nieces are coming for a cookout before school starts. I will need to get moving early in the morning to get some cleaning done and prepare the cook site. It'll take a bunch of coffee to ward off this chill in the air.

Rain! We've had rain! *Wonderful, amazing, awesome, fabulous rain!* Get the picture? We felt unworthy when those first raindrops came, but how we praised God. The lack of rain was a good lesson for us. Now it seems to rain so easily. We should mow the grass every three days. The corn and hay are growing like crazy and looking amazingly different than several weeks ago. There is a lot of corn that is permanently damaged. It really depends on when it was planted. The weeds grow too. I don't remember ever seeing so many weeds in the pasture, fencerows, and cornfields.

Fall

My mind is filled with many thoughts this morning. Writing my thoughts is soothing to me, so maybe I can find some peace. First and foremost on my mind is Wayne's mom. In April she was a very sick woman. She pulled through with flying colors, although she had a colostomy. Now four months later she had reversal surgery. The surgery and recovery at the hospital went well. She was released, but two days later she was miserable, admitted to the hospital very sick again. They did surgery again at midnight, as the reversal was failing—filling her with poison. She needed a colostomy again. About an hour after surgery, she had a cardiac arrest. Heroic measures from the staff overcame that.

It has been a trying time since, as she battled a severe infection and her incision didn't heal. She's at the hospital with family members taking turns staying with her and Wayne's dad.

This is also the same time of year my mom got sick, and that's bringing back a lot of memories. It's now four years since she passed away.

◇◇◇◇◇

This time of year is filled with silage chopping, hay making, and fall gardening. It's corn harvest time too. Indeed this is always a stressful, busy time of year. Wayne wants to fill our silage bunker this week. They want to open the fields on Thursday evening after work and then really push it on Friday evening and Saturday. That will mean late nights, no routine, and fixing a lot of food for the men who help us. The biggest stress for me is the fear of equipment breakdowns, which means money for repairs, plus taking so much longer to get the job done. I tell myself to be more optimistic, but the pessimistic side of me battles for steady ground.

I really should make out menus and plan on what to bake and when it needs to be baked, so I can keep the cookie jar filled for the men. It's always easier for me to cook and bake once I've decided what I want to make.

In July we wondered if we would even have a harvest; now we feel abundantly blessed. Those rains were a saving grace for the crops. It is, of course, not like a normal year with moisture at all the right times, but it's some corn and hay nonetheless.

◇◇◇◇◇

My garden is looking abandoned and forlorn. Popcorn, carrots, peppers, tomatoes, and some late beans and lettuce are all that remains. I didn't get much of anything to can except peppers. Those produced by the gobs once the rains came. I really need more tomato juice, and I'm beginning to panic that more tomatoes won't ripen before the frost. I have enough salsa and marinara sauce, but I haven't canned any ketchup or taco sauce. We eat a lot of chili and tomato gravy during the winter, so I really need more juice yet.

Tomato Gravy

Talking about tomato gravy...My favorite way of eating tomato gravy is on fried potatoes. I thinly slice potatoes, like potato chips, and fry them. For some reason I think it is better this way than on hash browns. My family also uses saltine crackers crushed on their plates and then covered with gravy. I grew up using bread instead of crackers. This is a tummy-warming meal in the wintertime.

We haven't seen the sun on this chilly fall day, but it's been a pretty day anyway. A busy day, as any Saturday usually is here on our farm. I got up with Colleen at 2:00 this morning to throw things in her lunch pail as she had to go to work early today—her eighteenth birthday of all days. It didn't take me long to find my way under those warm covers again. I couldn't sleep right away though. I felt guilty knowing how hard Colleen would work before I would even start my day. I prayed for her until sleep overcame me. The snooze button then got hit way too often before I finally heeded the alarm's call.

We enjoyed a leisurely breakfast of sausage links, tomato gravy, and huge mugs of homemade cappuccino. We were a bit too leisurely to begin with because then we had a hard time getting into the right gear for the rest of the day.

It was Jolisa's turn to go to town with Ida, so she had the privilege of skipping the weekly cleaning chores. Karah and Emily helped really well with the cleaning, and we were done before noon. While I made a light lunch, Karah baked a chocolate cake. She baked it in two round cake pans with intentions to decorate it for Colleen's birthday. Emily whipped up some Rich's topping and Whip'n Ice to use for various dishes in the next few days. They blew up balloons and put those, along with birthday cards and a sign, up in Colleen's room to surprise her. To top it off, the flower lady brought a bouquet of flowers we could add to Colleen's collection of surprises.

When Colleen came home from work we hurriedly put the cake in the pantry so she wouldn't see it yet. She put her things away and went upstairs with the girls following close behind. When she came downstairs, she wanted to retrieve an item from the pantry. Karah and Emily's anxiety levels skyrocketed! I quickly volunteered to get her what she wanted, and at the same time Karah and Emily both said, "Don't go in there!" Their giggles exploded. Colleen guessed we were hiding a cake in there, but mum was the word.

After a quick lunch, I layered the cake with Whip'n Ice, and then frosted it with a thick layer of chocolate frosting. Karah then decorated it. She had a lot of fun. The girls helped me clean up the kitchen, and then I told them the afternoon was theirs but they had to keep the noise level down so Colleen could take a long nap. They promised they would.

◇◇◇◇◇

After five-and-a-half weeks at the hospital, Wayne's mom is now at home. She takes a lot of care with the incision not healed. I wish we lived a short bike ride away so I could go help every day, but the 10 miles is an hour's drive with the horse and buggy. I try to go at least once a week. Hospice and the county nurse also help. We continue to pray for her healing.

◇◇◇◇◇

Let the snow fly! I have in my possession the new Northern Indiana Amish Directory to keep me occupied for quite a while. The cover is a pretty brown color with gold script...very tastefully done. Now the inside is clean white paper—940 pages chock-full of interesting information. For some it was probably very hurtful to see their family in print with a loved one listed as deceased. I know it affected me in a way I cannot describe. So many changes occurred in the five years since the last edition was printed.

One of the main interests to me is names...and the combination of names a family chooses. Many choose names from a common ground—Bible names, for instance. Some have no rhyme or rhythm. Several years ago I printed a small book with names used by the Amish. Now I am upgrading that again. I've added a lot of new names.

When we were trying to decide on a name for Karah, we decided to add the "h" because Wayne has a niece Kara. This way we could maybe avoid confusion. I also liked the uniqueness it gave the name.

When naming Jesse, Wayne wanted to name him after the men he farmed for at one time. Their names were Jesse, Mark Alan, and Lee Alan. So we chose Jesse Alan. Jesse's initials spell JAY, the name of my youngest brother.

Winter

I enjoyed our family Christmas gatherings once again. I enjoy them a lot more than I used to when the children were smaller. We had to get up so early to chore, come to the house, get the children up and dressed in their Sunday best, and make it out the door in time to get to my cousin's house when the rest did. Not to mention the food that had to be fixed. We'd come home with tired, dirty children who didn't feel very good from all the sweets they ate and juice they drank. Mom was no better off, and I didn't feel like heading to the barn to do the milking again. Once I did get done with the chores, I felt a lot better.

Now I need to go walk at least two miles. I've also learned to leave certain foods alone and not drink any juice. That way I don't feel so bad. The children are now old enough to dress themselves, I don't have to remind them to brush their teeth, but I do still help the girls with their hair. And they do need to be repeatedly reminded to hurry out of the bathroom. One small bathroom with eight people, but we get by.

◇◇◇◇◇

Tomorrow I'll take hot lunches for the children and go to school. Two other mothers also participate. It's always a busy day, but I do enjoy it. I'll take a potato-and-meat casserole and dirt pudding. Hot lunch is always a highlight for the children and provides a break for the mothers because they don't have to pack lunches.

Jesse is bored right now. He's bringing me a book to show me things. Next he is snooping around in drawers trying to find things to dismantle. Next he eats a pack of fruit snacks. He keeps saying, "Mom!" every few seconds it seems. He's lit a candle for me. Now he decided to go bother his Aunt Ida. Most days he can keep busy, but it seems when I am writing it bores him.

<>◇<><>

Five days a week I get out of bed at 3:20, fix Colleen's lunch, and then slip back into bed until Wayne's alarm goes off at 3:45. I make breakfast, coffee, and fill Wayne's water jug. We pray together and then I go to bed again. Ridiculous. I really should stay up, but my true nature of not being a morning person shines through.

One morning at 4:30, my sister Ida knocked on my bedroom window and told me the horses were all out on the road. *Oh no!* I yelled up the stairway for Brian and Karah for help. I knew there was a lot of traffic on the road that time of the morning. Lord, please help us! I slipped on a coat, scarf, and boots and headed out the north door. Luckily I got them headed back, and the rest helped herd them in without much of a problem. Ida had stopped a truck, and the fellow patiently waited until the road was clear. My lungs hurt that entire day. I'm not used to jumping out of bed and hitting 80 miles an hour in the cold, early morning air. I did not go back to bed again.

<>◇<><>

Once the girls get home from school, Karah and I need to go get her new Sunday shoes. It's amazing how when one mentions the fact that she needs new shoes, immediately two others are also in dire need of some. They didn't holler too loudly this time because Emily just got a pair of new school shoes and Jolisa a pair of Sunday shoes.

<>◇<><>

Jesse loves playing in the snow this winter. The other morning he was outside playing well before daylight. He and our black Lab, Jacob, are best buds. Jacob has been opening the north porch door every time we forget to lock it. He loves to come inside and knows exactly where the cookie jar is. He understands many things about us, including our routine. I dare to disagree that dogs cannot understand us or that they cannot feel emotions. But as smart as he is, I do not need him in the house.

Year 6

Spring

As we enter into March, have you been able to keep your New Year's resolutions? I'm struggling, but I am not giving up yet. We don't have to expect perfection immediately, but an attitude of willingness will help us succeed. One of my resolutions was to reach out more to others around me. My thoughts often travel to my friends, neighbors, shut-ins…and the list goes on…but I don't let these people know. I am so satisfied at home and going about my own business, and that is important, but we are to help each other along life's way.

Sometimes I wonder where the fine line is of being too satisfied at home. I am a firm believer of Titus 2. We can read in Scripture of being "busybodies," and I have no desire to be labeled as such. Yet I do want to help others, to be available, to even just listen if that is what it takes. Friends have often carried me through rough times, and I want to be a friend, neighbor, mother, and sister like that too.

◇◇◇◇◇

On my birthday I was privileged to spend the evening with all my sisters sitting around my kitchen table. That was awesome! With Freda 800 miles away, that does not happen often. My brothers-in-law, my dad and Alice, my children, my niece Karen and her husband and son were also here. I made soft pretzels for everyone, and they brought snacks along. After going out for dinner, we sat around the table and the conversation flowed. We laughed until our sides ached. It was great. I really needed that.

That subject runs into my resolution of making healthier choices again. I have no desire to gain back the 60 pounds I've lost. But it was a treat to go out to eat, relax, and eat someone else's cooking for a change. Restaurant menus have healthy choices too. It's up to us to make the right choices. Sometimes I throw all caution to the wind, splurge, and then get back on track the next day.

For a long time I'd been dreaming of having an old barn beam put along our east kitchen wall to be used as a shelf. I was keenly reminded this fall at Wayne's niece's wedding. Wayne's brother had fixed up the reception area with old barn beams. I reminded Wayne about my dream. His brother even offered us a beam. I didn't bank on my dream too hard because I really doubted that it would happen. Shame on me.

Fast-forward to my cousin's house at our Christmas gathering. Wayne called to my attention the shelves they have in their entrance. They are made of rough-sawn lumber. I really liked those too, and agreed with Wayne they'd be much easier to build than the old heavy barn beams. I teased him about getting it done. His time is so precious, with working in the RV factory plus farming.

Well, one of the first nights the very next week, Wayne called me to come outside to check out the old wood he had found. Do I approve? I still didn't get too excited, but I did agree it was perfect. We put the plans together. A wide plank for the back, an eight-inch plank for the shelf, and we planned how he would make the braces. By then I did get excited!

The next day we had to go to town, so I got paint to paint that wall to ready it for the shelf. I painted it a brownish tan. On that Saturday, Wayne and Brian fastened the shelf to the wall. Yes, I love it. It is the old look I had in mind. The wall I am talking about is over eight feet wide, and the shelf is pretty much the whole width. The wall looks totally different. It was always just a bare wall where nothing stands along it. It always looked sort of forlorn. Now it looks cozy warm. Several teapots, some candles for light and warmth, a painting of an old Singer sewing machine and a quilt I did in memory of Mom now adorn that wall. Plus there are antique dishes from various sides of the family. We extended a pretty rod between the middle two braces where I hung a "double wedding ring" quilt wall hanging from Mom. This whole project made me lonely for her. She would have come over and watched the whole process and expressed her gladness that I'd gotten the shelf.

I beg forgiveness that I gave Wayne a hard time about my unbelief that he'd actually attempt a project like this. He's not incapable of projects at all. To the contrary, but he just doesn't have time for them. He fully supported my idea, and he is also satisfied with the finished project. We share an interest in antiques, furniture, and dishes, and we've been lucky to inherit quite a collection of both from family members from both our families.

Let me tell you just what a smart cookie my husband has for a wife. Observant about what's going on around me is not a natural virtue of mine. One morning upon arising at 3:50, Wayne observed the diesel engine was running to pump water. Upon arriving home from work around 1:00, he observed the engine was running but the air compressor was shut off. He thought surely this engine had not been running all day. But upon further investigation, yes, he believes that engine was running for at least nine hours.

Where was his smart cookie—me? At home, in the house, in my own little world. I had company for coffee and tea that forenoon, so in the morning I was busy getting the house ready. In the afternoon I worked on the north porch, the opposite side of the house from where the engine is located in the barn. I heard the engine in the morning when I went outside to check on some gates between the barns. I heard the engine when I went to the door to greet my guests soon after 9:00.

It simply did not register; I simply did not think about it. Smart cookie, indeed. I could dwell on the money burned that day. Diesel is expensive, as everyone knows.

◇◇◇◇◇

Brian went to a horse sale in the wee hours of the morning, so Karah and I did some of the chores. At 4:00, Wayne tried to explain to me how the gates are supposed to be moved after the horses are out so the feeder steers can get to their field. It didn't quite make sense to me, but I figured Karah would know. We thought we did everything right, plus I did some reinforcing of the gates so everything would surely be safe. Wayne later told me it wasn't quite like he'd said, but it worked and all was well.

◇◇◇◇◇

I harnessed a horse, fed the dog, checked messages on the phone at the phone shack, and headed to the house. The girls were doing their morning chores. Jesse and I got ready, hitched the horse to the buggy, and headed to Shipshewana. We were planning to meet my Raber aunts and cousins for breakfast at the Blue Gate Restaurant to celebrate my sister Leanna's fiftieth birthday. How I enjoy these celebrations! Heading north on SR 5 that morning, I began to fret with thoughts of doubt about having closed the coal stove. Leaving that door open would be a drastic mistake. I tried to mentally backtrack every step I took that morning. Did I or did I not? Oh great, a smart cookie indeed. I prayed for wisdom, and God gave me peace.

We enjoyed our breakfast and watched Leanna unwrap her gifts. I lapped up every minute spent with these intriguing relatives of mine. On the way home, Jesse and I stopped at the thrift store and the bulk-food store, and then we headed on home. We beat Wayne and Colleen home from their jobs. The coal stove was calm, correctly doing its business...the door closed.

◇◇◇◇◇

One Saturday night I was lying awake in bed. Jolisa was on the couch coughing up a storm. Sometimes moms lie awake at night. I wonder how many nights my mom couldn't sleep because of me. I guess I was busy deep inside myself because I did not hear a steer bawling. Wayne had been asleep when all at once he sat up in bed, quickly got dressed, and went outside. He put the steer where he belonged. The next day I asked him how he knew that steer was out of his pen. He thought it unnecessary to explain. Our instincts are different. Our observations are different. I notice other things he never thinks about. I hear my children in the night if they are sick. We balance each other, each bringing strong points from two different directions. And we shall call it good!

◇◇◇◇◇

Just having done our taxes and then receiving the papers in the mail regarding the amount of our property taxes makes me question our motive on trying to farm. Sometimes it makes no sense to me.

Now I sit down with a cup of coffee, a mug of water, and three pieces of Dove chocolates. The first chocolate wrapper tells me to go where my heart takes me. Okay, we thought our hearts were in farming, and we'll probably follow our hearts until we retire. Then the next wrapper reads, "Be a little mysterious." That fit right in. Farming expenses: cost of seeds, taxes, weather patterns, repair costs, and dead colts are a mystery to me. Why do we put ourselves through this? I don't know except some people just simply have it in their blood. I shall simply be submissive. Submissive without complaint...

This spring we lost two colts at birth and had two that survived. Brian and I declared no more raising colts. With Wayne working out, it is too much stress. A mare giving birth is a lot more critical than a bovine. Maybe by next April we will have forgotten the stress of the births this year and welcome baby colts to the farm again.

Then the skid loader died. It had hours and hours of use. If men could bake bread with a skid loader they would. We are in need of a new haybine too. Hey, what about the floor in the house? I'll wait another ten years. *Ahh*, submissive without complaining...

I did buy some paint. Six gallons to be exact. It was on sale at one of the local hardware stores. I bought one gallon at regular price and got the next gallon for five dollars. That was a great deal! With school out, one of these nice, warm, sunny days the girls and I shall begin. We will turn the house upside down and paint to our heart's content. And wash curtains, and doilies, and bedding, and carpets. We'll wash off the furniture and woodwork and scrub and wax the kitchen floor.

Wayne is way patient with me. I love to chomp on ice, and he doesn't complain about the noise. Sometimes he waits weeks until his pants are mended...literally. No, he hasn't had to go without—yet. He cheerfully eats whatever I set before him at the table, and he lives with all my shortcomings patiently.

He encourages me in my writing and painting. We discuss everything thoroughly from A to Z. He goes to town with me and good-naturedly listens to me tell people I love having him along to care for the horse, as if that were the only reason. He never complains how much I spend. He never has. He never questions my motive on buying something. I try hard never to give him reason to. So what if taxes are high and skid loaders and baby colts die? We have each other.

Summer

Sitting at the picnic table beneath two maple trees with the breezes blowing feels a bit cool. Pretty sweet for midsummer. Wayne and I just got done unloading three loads of hay. Seems with it being Saturday night, Colleen and Brian had better things to do with their friends. Karah, Emily, and Jolisa had other jobs to finish. Jesse flexed his seven-year-old muscles and helped me unload the bales. He was, well, not exactly in the way, but I practiced my patience with him being on the wagon.

The landscape is so lush and green with the vegetation growing like crazy. Our minds often travel back to the intense heat and drought of last year. Definitely a year we won't forget. Through God's grace we survived.

On June 29, at 1:30 in the morning, our family, all bright-eyed and bushy-tailed, settled ourselves into a 12-passenger van with a family friend as our driver, and we started on an 800-mile trek to northeastern Oklahoma. We had plans to spend time with my sister Freda's family for close to a week.

Ordering our breakfast at Cracker Barrel was a trip in itself. Our four youngest hardly ever eat at a restaurant for breakfast, and they had a bit of a time deciding what they wanted. We pulled it off with nary a hitch, enjoyed the delicious food, steered them past all those enticing gadgets in the lobby, and soon we were on our way again.

In the afternoon we enjoyed a short stop at the *Precious Moments Chapel** in Carthage, Missouri, marveling at Sam Butcher's talents. We arrived at Enos and Freda's house around 4:00 in the afternoon, ready to stretch our limbs and get some exercise.

We enjoyed an awesome week devouring many a s'more and grilled pineapple and bananas. We talked, laughed, and did just about all that goes with being at a sister's house with a fun family like she has. We had heated discussions on the amount of sugar in a 12-ounce can of pop, amongst many other things.

On Sunday we went to their church. Throughout the week we visited in many friends' homes. We went shopping a bit, went to the Tulsa Zoo, rented a swimming pool for an afternoon, and did laundry three times. The days were a gorgeous 80 degrees, the nights a cool 50 degrees, with absolutely no humidity. Those temps are almost unheard-of for Oklahoma at that time of year.

All too soon it was time to head back home again. We came home safe and sound on Friday night, July 5, around 9:00.

You should have seen Jacob when we opened the van doors! He would have crawled into the van had we let him. It was nice to be welcomed home.

Reality hit us straight-on the next morning. There were mounds of laundry to wash, green beans to can, a garden that needed attention after a week of neglect. It was back to the grind, and that felt good too. We can only vacation so long. No matter how much fun we had, our normal home setting is still the best. This is where we belong.

◇◇◇◇◇

We've been busy as usual, with more deadlines than normal. The next two weeks we have weddings that we are involved in, and then we have a wedding every other week until sometime in October. Seven weddings that I am to help cook for. These are highly anticipated events for our family. Colleen is server in several of these weddings, so we have been busy making new dresses for her and also for me as people involved wear certain colors...colors the bride picks out for us. Jesse needs a pair of pants to match his Sunday suit coat, plus several pair for school. My baby is in first grade. I have to admit he is not a baby anymore. At age seven, his brain is ready and in dire need of academic stimulation. I can tell it is high time for him to begin with his formal education. He is a builder, making many paper airplanes, canoes, taking apart any old toy tractor or equipment and rebuilding it into something different. He always is looking for something to take apart. Sometimes he took things apart his mom and sisters weren't too happy about.

I am having a hard time getting to the sewing machine this time of the year. I have ordered four bushels of peaches to can. Too bad they don't come to the door already in cans. I also froze a lot of peaches in single-serving containers for the children to put into their lunches.

This summer when we picked the black raspberries, I didn't have time to process them so I stuck them in the freezer. Last week I organized the freezer and decided I might as well process them now. I made 13 pints of jelly and 9 quarts of pie filling. It can be such a purple mess, but once I sink my teeth into a piece of homemade bread slathered with black raspberry jelly I quickly forget about the purple mess.

I also canned chicken bits and broth last week. I cooked 40 pounds of chicken for that. That'll make us some good chicken and biscuits or chicken and noodles. It is such a grand satisfaction and convenience to have those foods in the basement. We are so richly blessed.

Year 6

Fall

After coming home soon after lunch from helping get ready for a neighbor girl's wedding, I am puttering around here trying to do some odd jobs. I brought in the laundry and folded it. The girls will put it away when they come home from school. I tended our baby, and he is now peacefully taking a nap.

Our baby—a boy—came to stay with us soon after school started. Just like all babies, he changed our household being a bit domineering. I am not too impressed about his coming, but as always I swallow and give up my self-will.

You see, this newcomer is another puppy. A puppy in the house! I am still not completely accepting, but I am completely outnumbered, so I might as well make the most of it.

My agreement was the fact of responsibilities. Who will volunteer to clean up his messes if he has an accident in the house? Who wants to take him outside at 3:30 in the morning because he has to go? Who is going to train him to start with? I heard choruses of "I will," but for some reason with mom home all day, where does the responsibility lie? And if he does have an accident in the house when the children are at home, they still yell, "Mom!"

For the first time in 19 years I was enjoying my forenoons of freedom. Now I am back to potty training. My family says I will fall for him yet. They probably know what they are talking about, but I am going to pout about it for a while anyway. We named him Cody, and he does seem to be doing well. He is just a wee little thing—a teacup terrier of some kind.

We do not have Jacob any longer. That was a sad day indeed, but for several reasons we had to get rid of him. We miss him and his being totally loyal to us. He was a one-of-a-kind dog, but only a dog. One chapter closes in our lives and another one opens. Such is life.

Forty-five minutes ago the schoolchildren came home, and, *whoosh!*, they are outside again. Before they went outside, they put their lunch pails away, changed clothes, snacked on watermelons and peaches, put the laundry away, and washed the dishes. Now they were headed to the barn.

They are totally impressed with their dad these days. Besides getting little Cody, he also came home with their very first pony, a two-seated pony wagon, and a harness. The harness and wagon were used, but they couldn't care less.

Emily said the pony, which they named Tony, is exactly as she always dreamed her pony would be. The children could hardly believe their good fortune. They truly appreciate this new venture and take total responsibility of the small horse.

Late fall is not one of my favorite times of the year, but there are things I do enjoy about the cold season. Hot soup is one of those things. Tonight Wayne, Brian, and I enjoyed bowls of tummy-warming ham-and-bean soup. Sometimes I make jalapeno-cheese cornbread muffins to eat with soup, but tonight we just had crackers.

I made chicken noodles for the four youngest because they think ham-and-beans soup is nasty. As each one came by the kitchen asking what we were having for supper, I had them look into the pot of beans. Once they let their disappointments be known, I pointed to the pot of noodles and watched their frowns turn to smiles.

Tonight Emily reminded me of a dish called "Hunting Chicken." Don't ask me why it is called that, but it's what my mom always called it. I cook macaroni in a quart of chicken broth and chicken bits and some water. I add salt and some chicken base seasoning. Once the macaroni is almost done, I add some frozen peas. In a cast-iron pan, I sauté chopped onions and bread cubes in butter until nicely toasted. I sprinkle some garlic salt on top for extra flavor. Then I put the macaroni in a serving bowl and top it with the bread crumbs. This is a fast and extremely simple dish that is totally kid friendly. Well, except I always find a small pile of peas beside Colleen's plate.

Another thing about winter is having supper at 5:00 and then enjoying a long, cozy evening in the living room with the family...maybe even playing Old Maid with Jesse, reading, or playing other games.

Flannel sheets on our bed is another thing I have discovered I enjoy about winter. I had a mindset I didn't need those, but as I age I find my body changing. Now these cozy sheets feel wonderful.

◇◇◇◇◇

This winter will go down in history for our community. We had a record amount of snow and cold. We missed many days of school and work. It was a challenge as a mom to keep everybody happy and content. The children spent hours outside in the snow if it wasn't way below zero degrees. They also spent time bedding down the calves. Wayne and Brian spent a lot of time doing chores, keeping water lines from freezing, and pushing snow—mounds and mounds of snow.

We always had wet clothes hanging over the coal stove, either freshly laundered or from the snow. What a winter! Now, please come on spring!

◇◇◇◇◇

Cody is house-trained now. Thankfully it did not take long at all. He loves to go upstairs and wake the four youngest children in the morning, much to their chagrin. We don't have a door on the stairway, so sometimes he goes upstairs to wake them long before they think it necessary to greet the morning.

Jesse usually comes back down with Cody, and they cuddle in the recliner or in front of the coal stove. One morning I heard Jesse tell Cody, "You are my best friend."

◇◇◇◇◇

Karah and I did a huge laundry this morning. I would have loved to hang the mountains of towels outside on the lines and watch them flapping in the breeze, but, alas, it is zero degrees. My boots aren't high enough to stomp through that cold fluff of snow.

Enter into our laundry-cluttered kitchen, and you would see Jolisa washing the dishes while Emily tidied and swept the house.

I fixed an egg sandwich for one, cooked oatmeal for two, and the other two had cereal for breakfast. While one was packing the lunches, the cheap tinfoil tore while she was wrapping pizza pockets. We were in a hurry, or at least I was, but there she stood telling me, "Look, Mom, look!"

In that time I had dumped a couple of peaches, was cleaning that up, and *looked* at that cheap tinfoil so we could move on.

Next, Jesse was checking out something in the freezer compartment of the fridge and somehow we bumped into each other. The egg I had in my hand landed on the floor.

I'm surprised at myself—how calm I remained. We didn't have a bad morning considering the size laundry we had to do. The children were ready and waiting on time for their rides to school.

Year 7

Winter

Jolisa went to town with her Aunt Ida. She informed me she has $14 to spend. I asked her what she was going to buy with her $14, to which she started giggling and stated, "Chocolate!" She's right on being a lady. Who wants to live without chocolate? I am all for healthy eating, rarely eating anything with flour and sugar, but chocolate? Well, let's just say I have a hard time saying no to that. Actually, it's even worse than that.

Big candy bars don't bother me unless the package reads Dove or Milky Way. I don't eat more than two or three candy bars a year, but put a bag of Dove chocolates in front of me and you'd better hurry if you want one!

Karah has accomplished a longtime dream of hers. She has sewn two dresses! She does well for a 13-year-old. I bought more fabric, and now I want to cut those, so she can continue in her venture. I am anxious to have her home from school so we can keep two sewing machines humming. Emily and Jolisa can do many jobs to keep the household humming smoothly. Sounds pretty fantastic, doesn't it?

Don't forget the Equal Rights Movement my daughters are very involved in. It takes a strong mom to keep everyone happy and well adjusted. Sometimes I simply do not have what it takes. I would have no power were it not for my Lord and Master, who provides if I ask. I continue to praise him.

This past winter I often dealt with frustrations I couldn't seem to get on top of. I called it stress. "Lord, help me handle this stress." "Take it, Lord! I can't handle it anymore." One day I had a very inspiring conversation with a friend who told me she *chooses* not to carry any stress. *Choices.* That's really what this life consists of. We choose how we deal with things. We have to choose how we deal with situations and then live with the consequences. Not that this was news to me. I simply had to be reminded. I can choose if I will let circumstances get me down or if I will take all circumstances and learn from them. Make the best of them. That is not always easy, and I struggle, but every day I think of the choices I have to make. Do I let stress bog me down or do I give it to the Lord?

So I just keep on smiling, never complaining that my 18-year-old refrigerator is running at 60 degrees. Yes, I've got life down pat. Not a word of frustration is muttered out of *my* mouth. I lied. I am so human, and every day I need a fresh dose of God's grace because I fail miserably. I also need patience to wait until we are able to get a new refrigerator.

Today I am feeling so privileged to be living on our humble little farm here in Northern Indiana. It's muddy and a bunch of things are so patiently waiting for us to repair them, but I just feel so blessed. My life is busy and full yet gentle and quiet, living in the country in a Christian community. Yes, we are so blessed!

Spring

After a gorgeous, warm spring day full of hard, physical work, I trudge to the living room with the full intention of settling myself into that comfortable recliner of mine. I put my feet up and bury my nose in a good book for several peaceful moments. Just having relaxed, I hear some earth-shaking screams coming from the girls' upstairs bedroom. I can hear their feet pounding on the floor, hopping from one bed to the next, and then more screaming. I get weak, imagining some huge, wild animal must have crawled from under their bed or, worse yet, a human predator. They are now screaming, *"Mom!"*

I quickly abandon my royal chair. My feet hit the floor, run to the kitchen to get the flyswatter (the only weapon I could think of), and head up the stairs. For some odd reason I figured I could kill a demon with a lowly flyswatter.

I find Emily swaddled in a blanket and Karah, always the practical one, pointing to a huge bug. "Please get it!" she cries. I suppress my giggles plus a little anger, and quickly shoo the June bug out the window. What a fuss over one little *huge* bug. I can't believe my girls.

◇◇◇◇◇

School is out! The first day they were at home all day, we decided to go to Glory Gardens, the awesome greenhouse a mile north of here. I biked and the children hitched Tony to the pony wagon. They all helped decide what flowers we wanted, and I appointed certain flower beds for each one to plant and take care of this summer. Jesse picked out flowers for a pot.

When we got home, Jesse promptly planted his flowers. The rest of us planted ours, coming up a few plants short. The three girls hitched Tony to the wagon again and went to buy what we still needed. We planted the last ones in the rain, well satisfied that the job was complete. I told the girls I'm sad we're done already because I love going to the greenhouse, planting all we bought, being surrounded by green grass, warm spring breezes, and birds heartily singing their songs.

I hear a lot of ladies saying their rosebushes did not survive the harsh winter. I've been watching mine closely, but I do believe six of the seven will survive. The seventh one was a younger plant, probably not as deeply rooted as the older plants. Colleen gave me a red tea rose for Mother's Day. Wayne gave me a yellow one...I think just because he loves me.

We all love roses and usually keep a fresh bouquet on the kitchen table all summer long. We have miniature roses too that make perfect mini bouquets to set by the sink window to cheer our day as we do our daily kitchen duties.

We always plant annual yellow daisies, annual blue salvias, and annual white alyssum to round out these bouquets.

Year 7

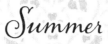

Summer

We have purchased a brand-new EZ Freeze Refrigerator! It is like a genuine Cadillac parked in our kitchen. We've never had a bigger fridge then 10 cubic feet; now this one is 15 cubic feet. It looks huge in the kitchen, but I think we will quickly adjust to it. It has a light and a huge freezer compartment. Yes, I love it!

Wayne looked in the freezer and commented on having this big a refrigerator and we hardly have anything in it. Just let me go to town, and I will quickly remedy that.

I probably sounded like a brat wanting a new refrigerator so badly, but I am glad we decided to buy new instead of repairing again because they found more things wrong than they had anticipated, and it would have cost us close to the price of a new, bigger one—and we still would have only had the small, old appliance. I felt that way from the beginning of the problems. Sometimes women do have good ideas. Did I deserve this new fridge? Absolutely not. I don't deserve anything. God is just so good!

◇◇◇◇◇

The county bookmobile was here yesterday, and now Jolisa is reading book after book to Jesse. He can read too, but Jolisa just loves reading out loud to him. She decided to join the summer reading program. She shouldn't have a hard time completing it as much as she enjoys

212

reading. I checked out some cookbooks to browse through. I think I am addicted to cookbooks. Colleen inherited the same weakness.

On to other things!

Dawn Dish Soap for Roses

Dawn dish soap is a staple in our house for more than just washing dishes. I've used it several years already to spray aphids on the rosebushes. The roses seem to love it, and it kills the aphids. I mix a half cup Dawn to a gallon of water and spray the plants thoroughly, also getting the underside of the leaves.

Dawn for an All-Purpose Cleaner

For an all-purpose cleaner: In a spray bottle, mix 2 cups water, 1½ cups white distilled vinegar, and ¼ cup Dawn dish soap. If the bottle is not full, add more water. That is the only cleaner I buy to use on the tub/shower surround, the kitchen countertops, the sinks (especially the stainless steel sinks because it gives them an awesome shine). The girls think the mixture stinks, but the smell quickly fades. And it is not toxic!

◇◇◇◇◇

Summer is marching by in grand fashion, but stepping way too swiftly to please me. Summer is always so fleeting, flittering by like the fireflies the children chase in the warm summer evenings. It seems those moments are way too few. It is so worth sitting around the campfire with our loved ones, relaxing and just being totally ourselves.

◇◇◇◇◇

For the first time in my life, I am the owner of a fishing license! Having only fished once before, 20 years ago, I was looking forward to spending a day on the lake. Wayne, Brian, Jesse, and I met Wayne's brother Merlin and his wife and son one morning on the lake to try our luck. I was already envisioning a fish fry! That's like counting your eggs before they are hatched. To my amazement, I caught the first fish! Even though it ended up raining, we half froze, and we hardly caught any fish, I really enjoyed the day.

◇◇◇◇◇

We also went camping, swimming, fishing, and eating at Wayne's eldest niece's place. They live within walking distance of three lakes, where we spent some very relaxing moments enjoying each other's company. We grilled on the pontoons and watched the bald eagles from our peaceful spot on the water. The children swam; the men and boys tried their luck at fishing.

Some skunks would have loved to join our circle around the campfire later that night. I think they smelled JoEllen's grilled bacon-wrapped shrimp. The girls and I thought we were so tired we could hardly move anymore. We were pretty well melted into our camping chairs when Adrian so calmly said, "Daddy, there's a skunk over there." We discovered we still had enough energy to move really fast.

We had borrowed a neighbor's pontoon, so a couple days later Karah and I went back there with Tony and the pony wagon to get our things. In the course of our chatting with the neighbor family, Dean asked us if we would be interested in a black Lab puppy. Karah and I looked at each other in disbelief. The children had been *begging* for another Lab dog, faithfully watching the pet ads in the daily paper and hoping to find one we could afford. We quickly informed him we most certainly would! He said they woke up the other morning to four puppies in their front pasture, and he has been unable to locate their owner.

Dean took us to the puppies. Karah fell to the ground, and those lovable dogs were all over her wanting to play. Typical Labs. These were in super shape; someone had taken good care of them. We gathered ourselves up, went home, and headed to the barn where Wayne was working to ask if we could get one. Within five minutes the four youngest were on the pony wagon again heading to buy a puppy! That was the beginning of our life with Charlie.

To begin with, Cody did not like Charlie at all. I think he was afraid of him because Charlie was so much bigger. After a few weeks, though, they were best friends; snuggling together to sleep and playing hard all day. Cody has grown a lot this summer, and I am waging war with my family. He will not return to the house this winter. He has Charlie to snuggle with, and he will be okay outside in the mudroom. This time I will not back down. I think they know I am serious, and I think I have Wayne on my side.

I did the laundry this morning while the girls packed their lunches and cleaned up the house. They helped me hang up the laundry on the lines after it was light enough to see. Before they were done, I noticed it was sprinkling and the eastern horizon was very red. Hmm, "red in the morning, sailors take warning." I remember seeing in the paper on Saturday that it was predicted to rain today.

We're having a typical Monday morning. After the four scholars headed out the door, I quickly gave the kitchen a last swipe through and decided I might as well go bring the laundry in and hang it under the porch roof. We've done that a lot this cool, rainy fall. My brain has been trying to grasp the fact that winter is on its way. I am rebelling furiously.

◇◇◇◇◇

On one of those cool, fall days, Colleen was baptized in our church in the name of the Father, Son, and Holy Spirit, and in front of the witnesses of our church family, some relatives, and friends. It was a small gathering, and so, so special.

The same day was the sixth anniversary of Mom's passing, which caused tears because of the closeness my mom and Colleen shared. Mom's sister Ida and her husband, Lee, and Mom's brother Ervin and his wife, Clara, came to share in our joy, which meant so much to us.

It was like a little bit of Mom was there. Colleen making the decision to be baptized in our church and becoming a member makes motherhood all worth it. Our children are the only things we can take with us to heaven, so we need to keep on keeping on, one day at a time, living for the Lord.

Another Note from Lena Yoder

With Wayne and I in our forties, Colleen is now 20; Brian, 18; Karah, 14; Emily, 12; Jolisa, 11; and Jesse almost 9. Our lives are so different than our early married life with farming full-time and having our hands full with little ones.

The Lord has handed us a huge surprise package! Javan Daniel, child number seven, was born in March! We are so blessed; the Lord is so good.

Glossary

Bulk tank: A large container for storing raw milk.

Choring: Doing the various daily tasks required on a farm, including milking and cleaning stalls.

Commodity shed: An open-sided building with a high roof and, often, multiple sections for storing bulk livestock feed.

Conservo: Steam-cooker patented in 1907 by Charles Swartzbaugh. A rectangular metal box with an oval top and base of copper. It had two front doors and four metal grill-type shelves.

Cultimulch: To use an agricultural tiller and seed bed preparer.

Dunk eggs: Eggs over easy.

Foliar feeding: Spraying a water-based fertilizer on the foliage of plants.

Forecart: A two-wheeled cart for farm work that can be modified so various pieces of equipment can be mounted to it, such as a sprayer or hay rake.

Fresh heifer: A young cow that just had a calf. The mother and calf are separated: the cow becomes part of the dairy herd and the calf is bottle-fed.

Haflinger: A breed of horse that can be traced back to 1874 to stallion "249 Folie," out of a Tyrolean mare and half-Arab stallion. Also known as Avelignese.

Haybine: A hay mower that requires a cart mounted with a diesel engine to run the horizontal set of blades. Haybines also have rollers to crush the grass to aid in curing (drying).

Haylage: Forage that is essentially a grass silage wilted to 35 to 50 percent moisture.

Head gate: A metal gate that loosely closes around a cow's neck to hold the cow in place.

Jones Fruit: A family-owned brand of specialty packages of fruits and nuts available at our biannual consignment auction.

Long Johns pastry: Long, rectangular doughnuts with fruit filling.

Milk house: A structure for keeping fresh milk cold and isolating it from the smells, dust, and microbes of a barn environment.

Motor room: The room that houses petroleum-powered motors for running milking machines and other equipment.

Nothinz: A shoe brand, "unique and comfortable footwear made from a blend of light and durable polymer materials" (www.nothinz.com, accessed 2/17/15).

Parlor/milking parlor: The barn area on a dairy farm where milking is done.

Precious Moments Chapel, Carthage, MO, and Sam Butcher: The creator of Precious Moments figurines, Sam Butcher built a small park and chapel for visitors to enjoy. He painted the inside of the chapel with biblical scenes featuring Precious Moments characters.

TMR/mixer wagon: An agricultural machine used for weighing, mixing, and distributing feed for cows and other cud-chewing animals.

Unker's: Multipurpose therapeutic personal care salve, often with pain-relief properties.

Also by Lena Yoder

The Life of a Farmer's Wife
Whether telling the story of a runaway buggy carrying her children or recounting the normal chores of cleaning, baking, laundry, and milking, Lena Yoder draws you into the world of Plain living.

The Tastes of Farmer's Wife
Lena offers this collection of her favorite recipes for good, homemade food. Besides the recipes, which range from traditional dressing served at Amish weddings to chicken enchiladas, Lena shares hints and tips on household chores, including packing lunches, making your own cleaning solutions, and mixing up children's play dough.

The cost per book is $9.99 + $5 for shipping and handling.
To order these books, send a check or write to:

Lena Yoder
9120 W. 300 S
Topeka, IN 46571

The Homestyle Amish Kitchen Cookbook

Georgia Varozza

Let a Little Plain Cooking Warm Up Your Life

Who doesn't want simplicity in the kitchen? Most of these delicious, easy-to-make dishes are simplicity itself. The Amish are a productive and busy people. They work hard in the home and on their farms, and they need good, filling food that doesn't require a lot of preparation and time. A few basic ingredients, some savory and sweet spices, and a little love make many of these meals a cook's delight. And if you want something a bit more complex and impressive, those recipes are here for you too.

Along with fascinating tidbits about the Amish way of life, you'll find directions for lovely, old-fashioned food such as

- Scrapple
- Honey Oatmeal Bread
- Coffee Beef Stew
- Potato Rivvel Soup
- Snitz and Knepp
- Shoo-Fly Pie

Everything from breakfast to dessert is covered in this celebration of comfort food and family. Hundreds of irresistible options will help you bring the simple life to your own home and kitchen.

Georgia Varozza has worked in the publishing field for more than 20 years as a journalist, editor, and writer. As a certified Master Food Preserver, she's taught many people in her community how to safely preserve their family's foods. Georgia comes from a Plain background, and many of the recipes she shares are family favorites.